QUALITY
VENISON

Homemade Recipes & Homespun Deer Tales

BY
STEVE and GALE
LODER

Dedicated To My Dad: Harry Loder

June 9, 1929 to December 3, 1993

My dad earned a living as a butcher in upstate New York when I was a youngster. Later, when in my teens, my dad's love for cooking took him into the restaurant business. Year after year Dad would cook delicious game of all kinds, but especially venison, for me and other customer friends at the restaurant.

When I became a deer hunter, my dad encouraged me to bone out my own deer, as well as giving me cooking and freezing tips. He emphasized freezing lean, nutritious venison trimmed of all fat, tallow or bone. Later I learned that double wrapping my treasured venison also helped preserve its taste and texture from season to season.

I was finally "brave enough" to begin boning my own deer in the early 80's after studying "Boning Out Your Deer" reprinted on page 26. Since I also have control over my venison's aging process (plus trimming and freezing), by boning it myself, the quality control makes a big improvement in my family's venison year after year.

Thanks, Dad. I know you would be really proud of the son I have become. As Dad would like it, over the years I have been hunting, I have also developed a joy for cooking all wild game and especially venison. Try our quality recipes on your quality venison.

Enjoy!

1st Printing, 2,000 copies   5th Printing, 5,000 copies
2nd Printing, 2,000 copies   6th Printing, 4,000 copies
3rd Printing, 4,000 copies   7th Printing, 4,000 copies
4th Printing, 5,000 copies   8th Printing, 3,000 copies
9th Printing, 4,000 copies

ISBN: 0-9662284-0-5

Copyright © 1998
Published by Loders' Game Publications, Inc.
P.O. Box 1615
Cranberry Township, Pennsylvania 16066
(724) 779-8320

WIMMER
COOKBOOKS

ConsolidatedGraphics

800.548.2537
wimmerco.com

Respect the Whitetail Deer

The earth is precious to God, our creator. Native American Indians knew this and felt that to harm or misuse the land, the natural resources or its wild animals would heap contempt on its very creator. So the Indians lived in a spiritual oneness with all wild game who were living off the land as they were. The deer and all wild animals of the earth were respected like brothers. They were a gift from God.

We encourage all deer hunters to hunt safely, ethically and yes, respectfully, for venison they value for their family. Do not hesitate to share your "harvest" with the needy when you are blessed with abundance. It is a gift from God that is to be shared. Give thanks!

A special thank you to our daughter, Kelly, "★", for her creative illustrations that are strategically located throughout this printing of *Quality Venison*.

On the Cover: "In Thanksgiving"

Limited Edition Print
painted by Jack Paluh

All wild creatures were gifts from The Creator and the harvesting of these animals by the Eastern Woodland Indians was motivated by survival. Animals were believed to be of the same spiritual kingdom as the Indian Hunter and were honored for their courage, strength and beauty. As these Native Hunters deeply respected nature, to extinguish such a gift was not taken lightly.

In Thanksgiving the woodland hunters, following the Beliefs of their Fathers, ceremoniously sprinkled tobacco over the harvested animal. They reverently spoke in honor of the deer's memory and gave thanks to The Creator for the gift of food. This sacred custom was believed to release the animal's spirit back to the harmony of all nature.

Jack Paluh, Artist

After fifteen years of concentrating on the abundant beauty of our woodlands, Jack Paluh has ventured into new territory. This new pursuit is to represent the hunting and fishing skills of the Eastern Woodland Indian. It was their devotion to the hunt, their sensitivity to the land, and their intimate understanding of nature that has inspired Paluh on this new venture.

"I am fascinated by these Native Hunters," states Paluh. "Their hunting was an art motivated by survival. To be able to hunt successfully, the hunters needed endurance and patience along with a steady hand, a sharp eye, a swift foot and a strong arm. These skills enabled them to survive in a harsh land."

Storytelling still reinforces the paintings of Jack Paluh. "My goal," says Paluh, "is to share an experience with my work and tell the story of that experience. I would like to inspire in my viewers a new awareness of our environment and the wildlife that surrounds us today and of years ago. We are the Caretakers and how well we manage these God given gifts will determine what we pass on to our children."

For more information on artwork by Jack Paluh, contact Jack Paluh Arts, Inc. at (814) 796-4400.

Welcome To Steve's Kitchen

Preparing deliciously nutritious wild game of all kinds has been a tradition in our family's restaurant in upstate New York and on our dinner table for over thirty years. It was through my dad that I learned the importance of quick cooling and proper field dressing of wild game, especially the whitetail deer.

In his restaurant Dad excelled in preparing savory wild game dishes especially when it was my venison. Dad knew I had carefully field dressed the deer and we had aged the venison properly according to temperatures. We would always patiently trim and bone out my venison before being double wrapped for freezing.

Great venison recipes are easy with quality cared for venison from the field to your freezer!

Acknowledgment

When we look back over the way our venison cookbook was conceived, and the way it will be marketed and sold, we see our Lord's guiding hand. With our book's successful sales we want to give a tithe amount back to the Catholic Church, Catholic Charities, and other Christian organizations who are helping the less fortunate children of God here in our country and around the world.

We thank you, oh Lord, for all you do for our family!

To Your Health

Contributed by Dr. Donald Mantell, M.D.

Today more and more Americans are becoming diet conscious. A diet high in fats, calories, and cholesterol may lead to heart disease, certain kinds of cancer and often obesity. The amount of cholesterol that accumulates in the blood steam over time is affected by the fats you eat.

Cholesterol is the fatty substance contained in red meat, poultry, fish and even wild game. Saturated fats are found in meats, dairy products and tend to become solid at room temperature. Unsaturated fats tend to stay liquid at room temperature and are classified as either: monounsaturated which are those found in plants, animals, and seafood or polyunsaturated, such as those found in vegetable oils.

While fats are necessary in the diet to make your food taste good, eating too much fat of any kind is not a good idea since all fats are high in calories (45 calories per teaspoon).

To maintain your healthy levels of cholesterol in your bloodstream you need to be aware of what kinds of fats you eat and cook with, too. Generally, cooking with oils with unsaturated fats will help lower your cholesterol level, especially if you combine a low fat diet with regular exercise.

Why would you eat Venison vs. Beef for your health?

Wild deer are naturally more lean and active than domestic beef. A deer's diet is free of additives to color meat. In addition, venison also does not contain the synthetic hormones used to increase the rate of growth of beef or any antibiotics. Venison is also good for you because it has less calories, less saturated and monounsaturated fats, and has slightly more protein than beef.

Ministering With A Meal

By Gordon Krause

Funny the things that stick with you. Back when I started college some twenty odd years ago, students were forced to take mandatory elective classes in addition to their major, mine being Computer Science. Searching the catalog, I hit upon "Psychology 101." Great! Sounded like an easy-to-pass course that might even provide some secrets about how people think. Well, I did pass the class, but sorry to say, have forgotten most of what I learned. However, one lesson stuck with me after all those years. It was about the Pyramid of Needs that all men and women have. Roughly stated, everyone has a pyramid of various needs, the lower layers necessary before the upper layers can be built upon. The lower layers contain things like food, shelter, clothing and security, the basic daily needs we all take for granted. The upper layers are concepts like love and spiritual fulfillment. The premise is that it is impossible to reach the upper layers if there are serious problems with the lower ones. In other words, you probably will not be putting much thought into your spiritual growth path when you are cold, hungry, homeless and afraid of being harmed on the streets.

That made good sense, and recently it occurred to me that Jesus probably knew all about this concept long before the word Psychology had even been invented. Take a look at how food played a big part in many of the situations that Jesus found himself in with his followers. The loaves and fish that he fed to the multitudes, the wedding feast of Cana, and of course The Last Supper. It's as if Jesus knew that a person free from hunger was going to be much more open to the "Word." At FHFH, we can help to do the same. No, we don't require anyone to listen to a sermon before venison chili is served for lunch. But by helping to fulfill the basic needs of the people that receive our venison donations, we build up the lower layers of their pyramids, allowing them to climb up to where they can hear whatever ministry they are exposed to. By supporting FHFH in time, talents and treasures, we can all be indirect ministers of the healing "Word." The "Word" we all so desperately need to hear! (For information about this program call 301-739-3000 or log onto their Website at www.fhfh.org.)

Introduction

When was the last time you heard someone say: "Oh, I don't like to eat venison because it is too gamey for me." I always feel sorry for anyone who feels this way. But I can understand why, because at their last venison meal the hunter and the cook may have pooled their lack of knowledge to place a gamey venison meal on the table for their guest.

It is possible the hunter had not learned or knew how to best field dress his deer for the table. It made the venison worse if the hunter left the deer carcass uncovered and exposed it in the bed of his truck for a few days, exposing it to the elements and noxious car and truck exhaust, as he drove a few hundred miles home. At what temperatures was the venison aging taking place and how long was it before the boning and freezing of the venison took place?

Perhaps the cook did not learn or know how to butcher and prepare very lean, nutritious venison. Furthermore, the cook may not have used the best seasonings for venison's rich flavor. Careful control of cooking time and temperature for venison is also very important. Therefore you may have a reason for the bad taste venison last left in your mouth!

Venison — when properly cared for — is both delicious and nutritious! The purpose of this field-to-meals cookbook is to illustrate the best way to field dress and skin your deer. It will also give a practical illustrated guide to boning your own deer, aging and freezing your venison as the quality meat that it is. This hands on quality control of your venison from several days to a week after taking your deer makes all the difference in your venison's taste quality meal after meal, year after year. You also can take whatever venison cuts you want to your favorite butcher for venison ham, hot sticks, hot dogs, salami, etc. You control getting all your own venison into your freezer between what you bone out, trim and freeze and what your butcher processes and returns to you. Sounds like you are getting the most quality venison out of your deer to me!! What do you think?

Table of Contents

◘ What If I Need A Taxidermist?

So you have taken your first and hopefully not your last buck as your trophy and you want to have it wall mounted by a good taxidermist. Let me share some tips with you from what I learned from getting my 9-point buck mounted.

Since deer hunting is unpredictable you would be wise to do all your taxidermy research completely one time before deer season and then recap your taxidermy needs prior to each deer season to see if circumstances have changed. As you would for anything expensive, shop for the taxidermist who will guarantee the best quality mount for the price you are willing to pay. Taxidermy quality and prices vary widely. So always examine the taxidermist's work in his office or home, get referrals with their phone numbers and a deadline when your mount will be done.

You want to be confident that if you take your trophy buck to be made into a trophy that it will be mounted professionally so it looks alive and memorable for years to come. Now with the taxidermy decision made patiently and logically you can concentrate on all the other matters at hand during the coming deer hunting season.

Girth, Weight Conversion

While in the field I carry a cloth measuring tape with me to help me estimate a harvested white-tailed deer's weight.

By measuring the circumference of a deer's chest (this is the girth behind the front legs) I can closely determine its "live weight."

A 28-inch girth is equivalent to approximately 85 pounds. A 32-inch girth is approximately 110 pounds. A 36-inch girth is around 145 pounds, and when you get to 40 inches get some help to drag him out. He's a brute in the 180-pound class. Simply use a pen to mark on your cloth tape each increment so it will always be there.

This method of "taping a weight" is commonplace in the livestock industry. You can also use your tape to measure a buck's antlers.

⊡ Caping Your Buck For Mounting

It is safe to say that most deer hunters dream of one day taking a buck that is large enough physically and that has the multi-pointed rack worth having wall mounted. Be it as a result of plenty of time on stand year after year or just beginner's luck, most hunters will eventually take "their" trophy buck. When you do:

It is not necessary to cut a deer's throat during field dressing to bleed the deer and this cut would also completely ruin your deer's cape for mounting. Do not cut its throat.

Be careful dragging your deer over rocks, logs and other forest debris because it can scar the sleek trophy hide around its front shoulders again ruining your trophy mount.

A great suggestion is to cape your buck as soon as possible after hanging it by its hind legs to begin its cooling and venison aging process. A deer's cape can sour if left on too long, causing the hair to soon fall off the hide. This hair loss (falling out) can happen within 12 to 24 hours in warm weather again ruining your hide.

Simple Caping Tips

After hanging the buck by its hind legs, use a sharp hunting knife to slit the buck's hide straight up the spine from the base of the skull to a point between, beyond its front shoulders.

At right angles to that first slice in the hide, make your next cuts on either side of the hide of the deer behind its shoulders. Now begin pulling the cape away exposing the deer's shoulders and neck.

You will have to cut the hide up the back of each front leg from its knee to the intersection of the earlier hide cuts. Then cut completely around each leg's knee.

Next cut the hide across the brisket in line with chest side cuts. Begin pulling the entire cape from the body of the deer carefully skinning it down to its throat.

Lastly saw off the buck's neck directly behind the skull. The head should be taken to your taxidermist of choice as soon as possible for his handling for your quality trophy mount.

✪ Skinning Your Deer

Reprinted by permission of *Outdoor Life Magazine* and Illustrator, Ken Laager, May 1997.
Dick Fagan of the Pennsylvania game department regularly demonstrates skinning for groups
of young hunters. He instructed the artist who drew these illustrations.

Here's an easy way to take the hide off your deer and prepare the carcass for butchering. With a sharp knife and saw, it takes only an hour or two.

A few things not covered below should be borne in mind. After skinning, it's important to cut out and discard all bloodshot meat around bullet holes. It is inedible and spoils quickly and may contaminate the rest of the meat. Pick off all deer hair on the skinned carcass. It lends a truly horrible taste when meat is cooked. The skinning method shown here results in a raw deer hide suitable for tanning and use as a vest or jacket. If you want to have a head-and-shoulders mount of your buck, you must "cape out." The cuts used for that purpose are shown in a circular inset in panel 13. For a detailed description of that process, see "Caping Your Trophy" by Michael Lapinsky, in *Outdoor Life's* Deer and Big Game.

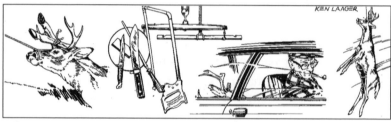

After gutting out, tie forefeet together over neck to streamline carcass. Drag out with rope around antlers and half-hitch around upper jaw. In vehicle, never subject carcass to heat. Don't use heater; keep windows open. Most hunters hang deer in cool place (41 to 45 degrees) for a week with the hide still on to tenderize meat and enhance flavor before they skin out and butcher.

1. With point of knife, cut hide from abdominal cut to just below both joints. Don't touch leg glands.

2. Skin out both thighs. Try not to cut meat or inner side of skin.

3. With deer still lying on the floor, skin out thighs to top of legs.

4. Saw off lower legs just below the joints. Use a meat-cutting saw or crosscut wood saw.

5. Hang deer with gambrel or stick in each leg between bone and tendon.

6. If it wasn't done during field-dressing, cut H-bone of pelvis with your saw.

7. Continue skinning. Leave tail on hide by tunneling under it between hide and back.

8. Hide in this area usually comes off quite easily. Pull on hide and then cut.

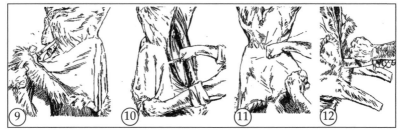

9. Sever tail near body inside hide. This avoids cutting the hair, which you'd have to pick off meat.

10. Use knife to separate hide from thin muscles near the abdominal lengthwise incision.

11. Hoist deer higher. Pull with one hand and "fist" hide.

12. Saw off forelegs. Split breast and neck and cut out the gullet.

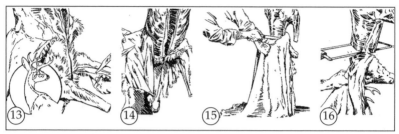

13. Slit skin of forelegs to the breast cut. If you want deer mounted, inset shows the cuts.

14. Skin out the legs and the neck. Neck is hardest area to skin.

15. Pull hide down and then use knife. Continue to base of skull.

16. Saw off head. Again, doing it this way avoids cutting the hair.

17. Clean carcass (see introduction) before butchering.

18. Hide still has head and tail attached. Cut head off. Wipe inside of hide dry with cloth.

19. Sprinkle borax or salt on inside of hide. Roll up hide, hair side out and place in plastic bag. Send package to the tanner immediately or store in refrigerator or freezer till you can do so.

◘ Venison Care and Preparation

After taking your deer, start to take great care of your delicious, nutritious venison by properly field dressing; then cooling it as soon as possible. It does not hurt to protect the cavity from insects or dirt, leaves, etc. by covering the cooled carcass with a cloth or other material to protect it during the trip from field to your kitchen.

Quality venison can start to be ruined during the field dressing stage or before it ever reaches the kitchen for boning. A deer's intestines and stomach contain strong acids which, if they spill onto venison can ruin it for any use. So it is essential to insure that these organs, as well as the bladder, are not cut during field dressing. (See "The Way To Quality Venison" on page 18.)

Whether you bone out your deer yourself completely, partially, or take it to a butcher, careful aging of your venison will give it its tenderness. Depending on weather conditions, use common sense about keeping the deer cold until it is skinned, quartered, and back tenderloins removed by putting it all on ice in two insulated coolers for your boning or brought to the butcher's walk-in cooler for his processing.

After I boned out my first deer and carefully trimmed it of all fat, tallow and double wrapped each package, my family enjoyed an improved venison flavor on every venison meal that year. I took all the credit for the improved quality flavor, of course, that I received from my wife and friends. In an attempt to be brief, when the hunter has the quality control decisions about how or when their deer is skinned, aged, butchered, and trimmed, he can put even better tasting venison on his table. It is plain and simple.

The most tender cuts of venison come from the inside fillet along the backbone, near the deer's tail, the tenderloin along the outside backbone and from the deer's hind quarters. The deer's front shoulders can be trimmed for recipes in a crock pot or cooking bag or ground to be used in venison sausage or venisonburger.

I can't emphasize enough that venison fat always has a strong flavor and it should be carefully removed, and bones removed before freezing your venison. Venison is very lean so before roasting it is often covered with bacon; oils or liquids are added to the recipe to keep the venison juicy during cooking. Fried or grilled venison is best medium rare.

The recipes included in this book are for deer camp or home cooking using the barbecue grill, oven, skillet, water smoker, or

Dutch oven. We have also included electric slow cooker recipes, having learned that this cooker is ideal for those recipes requiring long, slow cooking (venison ribs, stew, chili, soups, etc.)

Many standard recipes can be converted to electric slow cooker or crock pot recipes, especially those created for the Dutch oven. You will find that seasoning takes on a new dimension through this cooking process. Care must be taken to prevent strong herbs and seasonings from overpowering the other ingredients. Liquid measures, because there is very little or no evaporation, must be greatly reduced in this type of cooking. Reduce liquid volume about 30% generally from Dutch oven to slow cooker.

Did You Know?...

...Most bucks shed their antlers during December and January. Antler size depends upon heredity, age and diet.

...Age is determined by examining teeth replacement and wear.

...A deer eats about a ton of food a year.

...The most common method of deer habitat management is preventing forage species, mainly shrubs and trees, from reaching mature size.

...A piece of venison returned to the landowner who allowed you to hunt on his land may make you an especially welcome guest the next hunting season.

◘ Availability of Hunter's Venison

The most tender game comes from animals killed by surprise with a single shot. Once an animal starts to run, its muscles grow tense, and adrenaline spreads through its body, toughening the meat.

Proper field cleaning methods are essential to ensure that the game is safe to eat. Carefully remove organs and testicles. The gall bladder should be carefully cut away without breaking it, since if it spills on the meat or other organs, it will make them inedible.

Meat should be chilled as soon as possible after the animal's death and then should be kept cool by insulation until it reaches its destination. If meat is allowed to warm again after chilling, rotting may begin.

Large game (such as caribou, deer, moose, and bison) should be aged for 2 to 14 days (depending on type and size of animal) to tenderize the meat and enrich its flavor. Aging takes place at a temperature 40 degrees, within a total range between 38 and 42 degrees. If temperatures fluctuate much below that range, the meat will alternately freeze and defrost — a process that will ruin any meat. If temperatures rise much above the range, spoilage begins.

Commercial Venison

Both wildlife-protection and food-safety laws restrict the commercial sale of meat from America's wild animals. The only North American game animals that can be found readily in markets are those that have actually been farm raised, such as rabbit, bison, and some deer.

Selected supermarkets are beginning to carry venison in their frozen food cases. Many butcher shops can provide game by special order, and the number of mail-order game suppliers is rapidly increasing.

Game prices are still generally higher than the equivalent cuts of feedlot-fattened domestic meats, in part because free-range, organically raised animals take longer than feed-lot animals to reach salable weight. In addition farm-raised game is generally raised as a premium meat, without pesticides, insecticides, or growth hormones to fatten it quickly.

More important, for many thousands of years mankind has been selectively breeding domestic animals to furnish the greatest amount of meat — whereas game animals have been breeding themselves for the characteristics they need in the wild, such as speed and strength, rather than for rapid weight gain.

> *Ten years ago I read "The Way to Quality Venison" and I have found that using the information in it has been beneficial to putting delicious and nutritious venison on my family's dinner table every year since.*
>
> *It emphasizes good clean, one shot kills, proper and careful field dressing, cooling and proper venison aging, and the benefits of boning your own deer.*
>
> *There are even some venison freezing and cooking tips in it that any hunter can benefit from. The ideas in this article have worked for me and they will for you, too, year after year.*

⚡ The Way to Quality Venison

by Michael Stickney

Reprinted by permission of *New York State Conservationist* magazine, Nov-Dec 1987 issue. Michael Stickney works as a senior fish and wildlife technician at DEC's big game unit in Delmar. A native of the Adirondacks from Malone, Mr. Stickney now makes his home in Berne.

Another deer season has rolled around and soon many successful hunters and their families will be enjoying the fruits of the hunt done up in a favorite recipe. Yet there are others who will not savor the experience because their venison tastes bad or has spoiled.

It cannot be overemphasized that proper handling and care of your deer as soon as it is killed is the key to good venison. A good, clean, one shot kill is the first step toward ensuring quality. Hurried or poor shots generally mean poor bullet placement and ruined meat.

The most important thing is to get the carcass cooled down as soon as possible after the deer is dead. And the best way to ensure proper cooling is by proper field dressing and subsequent handling. A good knife with a sharp three and one-half inch blade is more than adequate for the job. Large "Bowie" or "Rambo" type knives are not recommended. They are difficult to control, and the risk of puncturing the intestines or cutting yourself is much greater.

A basic knowledge of deer anatomy will ensure that your field dressing will be done properly and with little or no mess. If possible, begin by situating the deer with its head uphill. Then roll it over on its back. Start your field dressing by cutting completely around the anus deep enough to free it from the pelvic wall. Pull the anus out far enough so it can be tied off tightly with a string to prevent feces from contacting the meat.

Now grab some belly skin in front of the genitals, pull it up and make a slit with your knife big enough for your fingers to fit in. Use your first two fingers, one on each side of the blade, as a guide for the knife point and to keep the belly skin separated from the abdominal wall. Finish the cut up to the breast bone. Now, with the same knife technique extend the cut from where you started back alongside the genitals to the pelvic area between the deer's legs. Peel back the skin to expose the abdomen. Then carefully make a slit in the abdominal wall so as not to puncture the intestines. Intestinal contents and fluids can contaminate the meat. Place the knife tip between two fingers of your free hand again and make the cut as before to open the abdominal cavity. Be sure to shield the knife tip with your two fingers to avoid puncturing the intestines.

Next, free the diaphragm, the thin muscle which separates the heart and lungs from the intestines, by cutting close to the ribs to open the chest cavity.

Now you must cut the windpipe and esophagus. Roll your sleeves way up and reach into the chest cavity to where the chest and neck meet. It is a good idea to maintain control of the knife blade with your free hand while preparing to make this cut. Since you will be going mostly by feel it is wise to know where that blade is at all times to avoid cutting yourself. Guide the blade to where the two tubes enter the chest cavity from the throat. Now let go of the blade, grasp both tubes and sever them with the knife.

Now you can remove the heart, lungs and intestines all at once with a little cutting of some remaining connective tissue. Be sure to remove the urinary bladder. It is a translucent sac located low in the abdomen within the pelvic area and can be taken out through the body cavity or through the enlarged opening where the anus and large intestine used to be. Be careful here. Spilled urine can taint the meat and affect its taste. Pinch the ureter (the tubes at the end of the bladder) and remove the bladder from the cavity and away from any meat before severing it and discarding the sac.

All that remains now is to turn the deer over, belly down, to drain the blood. Keep the chest higher than the hindquarters.

The deer is now field dressed. Put the heart and liver in a plastic bag (a bread bag works great) and drag your deer out of the woods.

Of course, many experienced hunters have their own techniques for field dressing deer. Some hunters remove the tarsal gland from the inner hind legs. Some remove the testicles. Actually the less these areas are handled the less chance there is of contaminating the meat. The tarsal glands are located on the surface of the inner hind leg not near any meat. Removing them is not recommended. If either hand or knife touches the gland and later contacts meat, the meat will be tainted with the glandular secretion. Also, before you go removing any genitalia remember the N.Y.S. Environmental Conservation Law requires that some proof of the deer's sex remain attached to the carcass.

Once you get the deer to the road and on your vehicle, prop open the cavity with a stick so air can circulate inside. When transporting your deer make sure you keep it away from engine heat. If it becomes necessary to carry the deer inside the vehicle or the trunk be sure to allow adequate ventilation, especially if the weather is warm.

Once at home or back at camp hang your deer quickly so the carcass will continue cooling. If the temperature is over 40 degrees, you should take the deer to a butcher right away for processing. Some people like to hang their deer to age and tenderize the meat. This is fine as long as temperatures are low and stay that way. Should the temperatures rise, the hide and hair will act as insulation and keep meat cold for a time allowing you an opportunity to get it cut up. This is true especially if the deer has been hung in the shade. However, do not allow the deer to freeze, thaw, then freeze again. If you are at all unsure about outside temperature have it cut and processed by a competent butcher as soon as possible.

There has been much discussion about the best way to hang a deer, head up or head down. Some believe the deer should be hung head down to drain blood away from the better cuts of meat. However, blood trapped in the cavity because of improper cleaning and draining can settle in the chest, turn rancid and taint the meat.

The same can happen if the deer is hung by the antlers or the neck. I have had equally fine venison from deer that were hung either way. The key is to make sure the deer is adequately opened, well drained of blood and cooled down quickly. Some people cut up through the brisket to open up the chest cavity. However, do not cut beyond the front legs if you plan to have the head mounted.

Most hunters have their deer cut up, wrapped and frozen by a butcher. You can usually find a reputable meat cutter through hunting partners who have had good results with a particular individual. The cost is not great but prices will vary with location. There are many people, however, who prefer to cut up and process their own deer.

Cutting up your own deer allows you to prepare cuts of meat to suit your needs, something a lot of butchers do not have the time to do. You can keep waste to a minimum by boning the meat out as well as trimming the different cuts the way you like. You not only make better use of freezer space when you bone out venison, you also eliminate bone marrow and tallow that can leave a waxy feeling in your mouth. If you would like to try your hand at processing your own deer or just reading about how it is done, refer to "Boning Out Your Deer," on page 26.

Remember that venison is a lean meat. Overcooking can dry it out and make it tough. Venison is versatile and can be prepared many ways from simple frying to gourmet cuisine, from canned to smoked and dried jerky meat. And remember this too, Venison has its own flavor. You should not expect that it will taste like beef or pork.

So this year, whether you take your deer to a butcher or decide to cut it up yourself, do it right from the start.

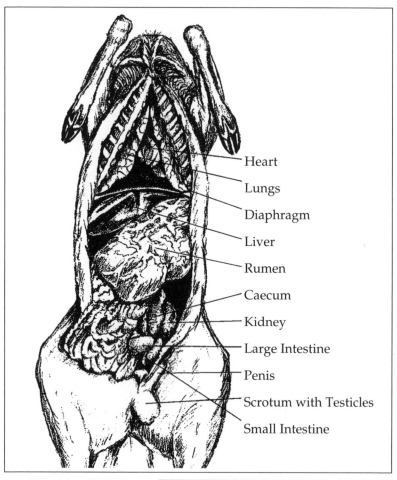

Heart
Lungs
Diaphragm
Liver
Rumen
Caecum
Kidney
Large Intestine
Penis
Scrotum with Testicles
Small Intestine

A basic knowledge of deer anatomy is helpful in field dressing. (above)

A good sharp knife guided between two fingers will assure that inner organs can be removed without tainting the meat. (right)

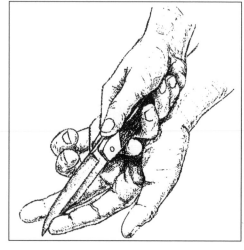

◘ How To Begin Your Deer Processing
And Other Tips To Quality Venison

Boning out or butchering your own deer is not difficult with sharp knives and after a bit of experience it can turn into a traditional, "labor of love," that gives the hunter some extra money in his pocket as well as much personal satisfaction for a job, once again, well done!

Here are some personal thoughts based on practical experience surrounding venison processing after your deer is harvested. They say there is more than one way to skin a cat. That can be said about the way to process your deer for the highest quality venison for your family's dinner table, too. But this is the proven venison method, of aging and boning that works for me and my family.

First, I am a serious hunter, but when I take a deer , experience has me quickly changing "hats" and "clothes" to become a quality conscious "venison processor". I prefer to skin a deer the same day it is taken and it will hang to age a day or two depending on outside temperatures. The next step is to quarter the deer to start the venison aging process.

First thing, with a sharp knife, remove the two inside venison fillets along the inside of the deer's spine between its hind quarters. Then remove the two venison loins along the outside of the deer's backbone. Begin this by placing your knife on one side of the backbone just ahead of the back ham or hind quarter, cutting down (about 2 inches) until you hit bone, then slice forward, using your other hand as a guide, to the front shoulder, keeping the flat part of the knife against the backbone just like you would when filleting a fish. You'll obviously see you are separating a boneless, prime piece of venison called the backstrap.

To completely remove it in one long 2+ inch thick strip, cut underneath it just on top of the ribs, keeping the knife against the ribs as you were doing earlier.

To separate the loin you will need to wiggle the knife tip in and around vertebrae to free small portions where the muscles still cling. Now place the fillet on a flat surface to remove any fat and the silver skin on the top of the loin — like you would, again, fillet a fish. Viola! Follow the same process to remove the other remaining loin and you are on your way. The fillet and loin are the very best cuts of venison on a deer so I always place them in a Dutch oven and age them in my refrigerator 7 to 10 days before cutting double wrapping and freezing this prime steak.

Now shoulders and hams or hindquarters can be boned while still attached to the carcass or after removal. I think they are easier to bone out if they are removed from the deer in one piece. First, take the front shoulders off by cutting venison between the shoulder and the ribs. Notice there are not any connecting bones. Next, detach the hams by cutting along the inside of the pelvic bone starting near the tail. There are some crazy twists and turns needed here. Do not worry, just keep cutting as close to the bone as possible until you hit the ball joint. Cut the tendons holding it together and the ham will come free. Same procedure applies to removing the other shoulder and ham.

After your deer is quartered you may want to use a meat saw or even a small hack saw to remove each side of the deer's rib cage. You can begin cutting at the stomach end along the backbone. It takes a little work for the amount of venison you get, but when time and freezer space allows, I will remove the ribs with a knife and a saw. I like to cut them in 8 to 10 inch squares so they fit nicely in a crock pot. Age the ribs in your ice filled coolers along with the front shoulders and hindquarters.

While it is ideal to age your quartered venison in plastic bags in say, your refrigerator, for a week or two it is not practical to most families. Having all your refrigerator space taken up for the aging period, as well as the boning and freezing time that is needed is not practical. So ten years ago or so I began aging my venison before boning and freezing it in large, quality, picnic coolers. They have lids, of course, and the venison is iced down and turned occasionally. Drain and add additional ice when necessary. I have never had venison spoil. It ages nicely and is never "gamey."

Place a front shoulder, one side of ribs, and one hind quarter (cutting the leg off at the knee) into a large quality cooler with lots of ice. In another cooler of ice, place the remaining shoulder and a hind quarter with leg cut off at the knee. Over the next 2 to 3 days, depending on outside temperatures, more or no ice may be needed to age your venison at what you feel are refrigerator like temperatures of 40 to 45 degrees. Use some common sense here to protect your venison's aging until you use "Boning Out Your Deer" on page 26 with its illustrations to bone out your deer's two front shoulders and hind quarters for venison roasts, venison jerky, stew meat, or ground venison for sausage or venisonburger.

Where does the venison come from that is used for ground venisonburger or venison sausage? It is bits and pieces accumulated from the neck, ribs, miss-cuts, and small left over trimmings that are saved when boning out your entire deer, etc. It can also come from the deer's front shoulders after they are boned out. Take any amount of your venison to your butcher to have custom specialties made from it or to have it ground up for the venisonburger and sausage that you can easily make yourself at home. Of course a little help from a hunting partner, your wife, or children during this venison processing period helps. It also starts a tradition of, hopefully, an annual event of preparing and freezing your venison for all to enjoy over the months ahead. Really, processing your own deer does become a "labor of love" and it will give a hunter much personal self-satisfaction when he enjoys delicious, nutritious venison meals because he made the effort to carefully and properly handle his quality venison from field to table.

Here is to your successful hunting
and even better venison eating!

Take heart! You cannot go too far wrong if you follow the step by step boning instructions in "Boning Out Your Deer" on page 26 to bone out even your first deer. And "yes" your deer processing gets easier with practice.

Tip: Sharp Boning Knife A Must

To make your job easy use a quality, sharp boning knife or two when boning out and removing all fat and tallow from your venison before it is ground up or frozen, double wrapped, in carefully marked packages.

"Boning Out Your Deer" was first reproduced nearly thirty years ago, but since a deer's anatomy remains the same it is still an invaluable illustrated guide to help you effectively bone out your own deer. It got me started. By boning out your own deer:

- You save money. Use it to have some of your own venison processed by your butcher into custom venison meats, jerky, salami, hot dogs, etc.

- You get to enjoy your own venison. After you bone out a deer or two, you will know what venison you want to freeze as steaks, roasts, stews, or ground by your butcher for venison sausage and venisonburger.

- You control the aging process of your venison, safe-guarding its quality, tenderness and flavor. You get to keep all of your venison.

- Your hand boned or processed venison will not have bone marrow from a butcher's band saw on it, or any fat left on it to taint the valuable and nutritious venison while in your freezer over the year.

- With each carefully and deliciously prepared venison recipe used all year long you will feel the pride that comes with supplying your family — with the very best quality venison year after year.

So with the help of this guide, you can easily bone out your own deer, and enjoy better tasting venison year after year.

◘ Boning Out Your Deer

By Andrew S. Landforce

Reprinted by permission of Oregon State University, Corvallis, Oregon, EB 819, Printed May 1968; out of print March 1993, 16pp.

The deer you've enjoyed hunting can provide many venison treats for your family. Their enjoyment of venison will depend largely on how well it is prepared for storage and how it is cooked.

This guide illustrates a method of preparing a deer for storage in your freezer and provides some additional tips on using venison. Removal of bones saves freezer space and improves the eating qualities of the meat. Cutting the meat into small pieces, as shown, makes it easier for you to remove tough connective tissue, fat, dirt, hair and bloodshot muscle. Bone-dust and marrow from the meat

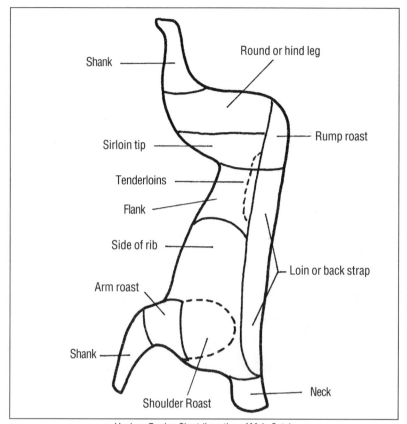

Venison Boning Chart (Location of Main Cuts)

saw are avoided and packages for freezing are boneless, compact, smooth and easy to wrap tightly.

The only equipment needed is a table top, a meat saw, a sharp narrow-bladed knife, a place to put the meat and scraps, and a little courage to tackle the job! If you have no meat saw, use a clean, sharp hand saw.

Carcass Preparation

Careful cleaning and quick cooling are important. Remove the guts in the field as soon as the deer is dead. While carrying it on the car, use a car top rack to allow air circulation under the deer, and prop the belly incision open with a stick.

At home or in camp, hang the deer by the head in a shaded place. This allows drainage. Clean the body cavity using cool water to flush it out as needed. Water is usually needed if the deer has been gut shot or if you accidentally punctured the intestine or bladder during visceral removal. Although water may hasten spoilage of meat hung for long periods, your deer will be processed and frozen within a few days.

Free the hide from the shot-damaged areas and cut away all bloodied flesh. If there is much of this, it may be soaked in salt water to draw out the blood; this meat may then be used for stews.

If the weather is likely to be near freezing for a few days, leave the skin on to keep the meat clean. Otherwise, make a cut along the belly from groin to throat, and slit open the skin on the legs. Start skinning at the head and continue down the body to the tail. Remove all legs at the knees. Trim off all fat, as it becomes rancid quickly. After hanging for approximately two days, the carcass is ready for boning.

Figure 1. The first cut is to remove a front shoulder. Lift the front leg up from the chest and cut the meat attaching it to the side of the ribs. Then work the knife back and forth to cut the connective tissue between the leg and the rib cage. The last cut to be made will be at the top of the shoulder blade where it is attached to the withers.

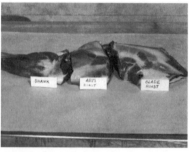

Figure 2. Cut the front leg into three parts — shoulder or blade roast, arm roast, and shank. (See Figures 3 through 6.)

Figure 3. Remove the shoulder roast from the leg by severing at the joint. Locate the joint by moving the shoulder blade up and down and then cut through it. Cut as shown in Figure 4.

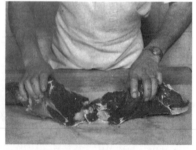

Figure 4. The shoulder blade roast is removed from the leg. Notice that the cut has been made through the joint. Trim the roast to make a neat-looking piece of meat. For roasting, the bone is not removed. The trimmings are good for hamburger and other uses. Also, for those who prefer steak, the muscles on each side of the bony ridge on the shoulder blade can be removed. These should be cut about 1/4 inch thick for frying.

Figure 5. To separate the arm roast from the shank, prepare to saw the leg bone by cutting the meat down to it.

Figure 6. Saw the bone in two. This is one of the few places where sawing is done close to meat. Trim the arm roast and it is ready for cooking or storing. Trim out the meat from the heavy tendons and tissue of the shank. This meat may be ground for hamburger.

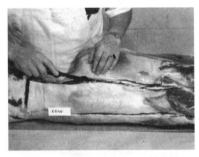

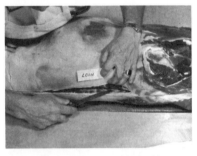

Figure 7. The back view of the whole deer with the outline of the preliminary cuts that are made in removing the loin or backstrap from along one side of the backbone. Three basic cuts are made. First, cut the flank loose just in front of the hind leg and extend the cut all the way to the backbone. This is the cut shown on the left in the picture. Second, use the vertical spines of the backbone as a guide and cut forward along these until you reach the base of the neck. Third, make the side-of-rib cut directly over the point where the ribs curve down to join the backbone. The position of the knife is shown in the third cut in the picture.

Figure 8. The vertical spines of the backbone can be used as a guide in cutting forward to the base of the neck. Cut down to the backbone until the junction with the ribs is reached.

Figure 9. The loin lies in the groove between the junction of the ribs and the vertical spines of the backbone. Make the sides-of-the-rib cut directly over the point where the ribs curve down to join the backbone (Figure 7). Remove the loin by cutting it loose from the ribs. Lift the loin and start cutting and peeling it from the groove, continuing forward until loin meat ends or the base of the neck is reached.

Figure 10. One of the two loins from a large deer, ready to be trimmed. Lay the loin on the table and prepare to pull off fat, odd-grained meat, and tough tissue by starting at one end. Cut enough of the connecting strands to allow a good hand hold.

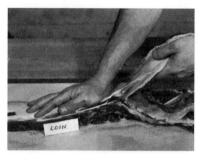

Figure 11. Pull and rip the layer of fat and connective tissue from the loin. The loin meat will still be encased in thin connective tissue. Remove the loosely attached meat near the neck end of the loin. This meat is good for stews, ground meat, or other uses, but it detracts from the tenderness of good steaks.

Figure 12. Cut the trimmed loin into steaks 3/4 to 1 inch thick. Loins are not very big, but have no connective tissue, off-grained meat, fat, or bone.

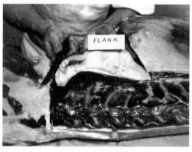

Figure 13. Remove the flank by cutting it free from the backbone and the adjoining ribs. The side nearest the hind leg should have been cut loose when making the first cut in preparing to remove the loin.

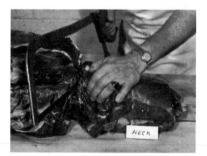

Figure 14. Remove the neck by sawing the backbone off just in front of the point of the shoulder. The neck meat makes excellent mincemeat, stew, or grinding meat. It can also be roasted whole.

Figure 15. Remove the side of the rib from the backbone. Use the saw and cut the ribs loose at the point where they curve enroute to connecting with the backbone. Cut all the way to the base of the neck. Good luck!

Figure 16. A side of rib that has been removed from the deer is shown here. You can either cut it up at this point or turn the deer over and start boning out the remaining side.

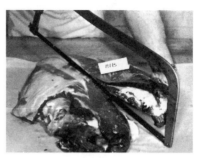

Figure 17. Here a side of rib is being cut into plates. Notice the layer of meat covering the ribs. It is usually left as shown, but the layer of meat can be removed and used for grinding meat, stew meat, or tiny steaks. Enough meat will be left between the ribs for barbecuing.

Figure 18. Plates of ribs can be barbecued whole or separated into two or three ribs per piece. If you prefer, ribs can be cut into short pieces and used in stew.

Figure 19. Remove the tenderloin by lifting and cutting it free from the backbone. The two tenderloins are located on each side of the backbone and just forward of the pelvic area. Each tenderloin is only about one and one half inches in diameter and a foot long. These are the most tender pieces of meat on the deer, and they are excellent for steak. To make the steaks larger in diameter, butterfly them. A butterfly steak consists of two steaks lying side by side and connected by the same tissue on one edge. These steaks are made by cutting the first steak almost completely off and cutting the next one completely off. Then they are folded edge to edge at the point of connection and laid flat in the frying pan.

Figure 20. (Pictured at left.) Saw the backbone off just in front of the hind legs. It can be cut into sections and used in making soup, or the scraps of meat can be picked off and used in mincemeat, ground meat, or for other uses.

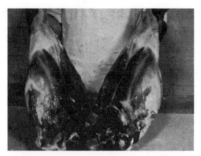

Figure 21. The two hind legs are ready to be separated by sawing through the middle of the backbone.

Figure 22. Use the spinal cord and the backbone as a guide in making the cut with the meat saw. Each hind leg is cut into a rump roast, a sirloin tip, the round, and the shank.

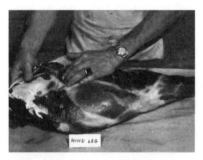

Figure 23. To cut up the hind leg, first remove the rump roast. To do this, locate the ball and socket joint which connects the pelvic bones of the rump roast with the large leg bone. Feel for the joint as you raise and lower the rump roast. Once located, cut as shown in Figure 24.

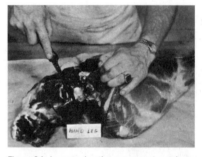

Figure 24. In removing the rump roast, cut down to the ball-and-socket joint and work the knife through it as shown above. Make the cut as vertical as possible, and yet leave enough meat on the rump roast for a meal. Separating with a knife instead of sawing avoids spreading bone marrow and dust.

Figure 25. The rump roast as shown from the top side. Remove the fat and sharp projections of pelvic bone, before cooking or freezing. If you prefer other cuts to roasts, the meat can be removed and cut into small steaks or used for grinding meat or stew meat.

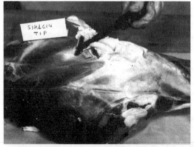

Figure 26. Next, cut the sirloin tip from the remainder of the hind leg. First, set the leg in a vertical position. Remove the knee cap by cutting it loose from the under side. If it is not easy to get the knife under the knee cap, cut directly down to the large leg bone which is shown in Figure 27.

Figure 27. Lay the hind leg flat on the table and remove the sirloin tip by using the leg bone to guide the knife while cutting off the large chunk of meat. Notice the large white bone in the meat. Start at the knee cap and keep the knife in a vertical plane against it, and cut the meat away from the bone with short strokes.

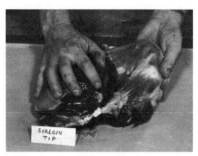

Figure 28. Once the sirloin tip has been cut from the leg, remove the connective tissue and extra meat surrounding it. The remaining chunk of sirloin-tip meat will be enclosed in a thin connective tissue and will resemble an undersized football.

Figure 29. The sirloin tip is excellent as a roast or it can be cut into thin steaks. The steaks should be thin if they are to be fried. Make them not over 1/4 inch thick. The meat is good for hamburger, stew, or other uses.

Figure 30. In removing the bone from the round, start by cutting the connective tissue that separates the shank from the round and the bone. Cut the tendon and proceed as shown in Figure 31.

Figure 31. Shave and cut the meat loose from the leg bone. This will take a little maneuvering around the joints, but keep cutting.

Figure 32. In this photograph, the leg bone has been separated from the large chunk of round. The next step is to separate the round into its individual muscles, each of which is enclosed in its individual envelope of connective tissue.

Figure 33. Divide or separate the large leg muscles in the round by cutting the connective tissue holding them together. Avoid cutting into the meat as much as you can. Notice the large ball of muscles held in the right hand. This does not make good steak meat — it is too tough. Remove it and trim out the meat for grinding or other uses.

Figure 34. Chunks of trimmed round that have been separated from the hind leg are shown above. These chunks can be made into steaks or roasts. For the smaller family, the larger pieces of round may be halved lengthwise. The round makes excellent steak meat when it is cut thin.

Wrapping, Freezing and Storing

Wrap all packages tightly in a double wrapper of suitable paper or seal in special freezer bags. Put a double layer of waxed paper between each steak. Label each package with the name of the cut and date. Draw a star on the better packages of steaks to be served on special occasions.

Spread the packages out in the freezer to freeze as quickly as possible.

Use venison within six to nine months for best quality. You need a state permit to keep venison after August 1 of the season following the kill.

Tips on Using Venison

Thaw meat in its wrapper in the refrigerator to hold in the moisture. Venison can then be cooked as you would cook low-quality beef, observing the following important differences.

● Since fat was trimmed off to avoid strong flavors, you may wish to add bacon grease or beef fat when cooking. Cover roasts with bacon strips for self-basting.

● Venison is often tough, so use moist heat cooking methods for all but the most tender cuts. Moist heat methods include stewing and pot roasting. Dry heat methods such as oven-roasting and pan frying should be used only for such tender cuts as loin, round, steaks and chops. All meat from an old deer should be cooked with moist heat methods.

● Venison is a sweet meat, so reduce sugar in sauce recipes. Use one-fourth less sugar.

● Do not overcook. Deer meat has short fibers that toughen quickly if overcooked or cooked at too high a temperature. Plan to serve venison medium to well done, never rare or overdone. Venison has a dark surface when roasted and may appear to be done before it actually is. Because of the short meat fibers, it is not necessary to pound steaks before cooking.

● Use your favorite shortening when frying steaks; bacon grease or beef fat are favorites.

● Venison fat is usually strong-flavored.

● Venison, like lamb, should be served hot.

● The boning process described and illustrated in this guide favors getting as many strips of lean meat as possible. The "steaks" are not always as tender as beefsteak because they may be cut from less tender muscles like the shoulder blade, the rump or rib ends. This will, however, make very good eating if cooked carefully. Serve medium to well done. Avoid overcooking or cooking at too high a temperature.

● Although freezing chunks of venison whole helps to preserve moisture, most cooks prefer ready-to-cook sized packages with steaks cut before freezing.

● Some families prefer to grind all or most of the deer meat, especially if the animal is old. Ground venison can be thawed and mixed with other meats for meatballs, meat loaf, deerburgers or deer sausage.

By the time I read to the picture in this article where the caption reads "We have charcoaled deer meat in snow, rain and wind ... but rarely miss a chance for one of these fine feasts," I realized I feel this way, too. There are numerous grilling tips including delicious charcoaled venison steak with only salt and pepper to season. That's all it takes to enjoy quality cared for venison and it does not toughen grilled venison as other sauces can. He recommends adding Worcestershire sauce or other garnishes to grilled venison steak one at a time and sampling it only after it is grilled to perfection. Look for the great venisonburger tips, too!

▣ Venison Needn't Be 'Pot Luck'

By Robert R. Bowers
Reprinted by permission of Pennsylvania Game Commission

The average American will overlook a tough and stringy cut of beef, and go back for more when his last pork roast turned out to be too fat. Unfortunately, such forgiveness has not been forthcoming when the first taste of venison didn't please the palate. Consequently, thousands of choice venison steaks and roasts go untasted and unappreciated every year, simply because of one sad experience.

Many of my friends who have never tasted deer meat of any description, maintain that they just don't like "wild meat." Others who, on one or two occasions, have been given a roast and hastily prepared it also

We have charcoaled deer meat in snow, rain and wind...but we rarely miss a chance for one of these fine feasts.

bear these same misgivings. Even members of my hunting parties habitually offer their deer to the first man who wants it. They can't seem to understand my anxiety to "bother" with a deer of my own or a portion of theirs. And my wife's friends shudder when she bluntly states that she hopes "I get another deer."

What most of my friends and fellow hunters cannot imagine is that we genuinely like venison, and that includes everything from the sirloin steaks and rump roasts down to the scraps which go into deerburgers.

What accounts for this distinct contrast in the eating habits of people? We like the same type of "store bought" meats. Are we kidding ourselves into thinking that we like deer meat, or is it that our taste buds differ greatly when it comes to wild meat? Neither of these possibilities is the answer. My family learned to like venison from experience. We didn't give up just because the first steak was too tough to cut, or the roast was too "green" tasting, We had bought similar cuts of beef and pork many times, but didn't give up these domestic meats on the basis of one bad experience.

For the past few years, my neighbor, Jack Willey, and his wife have agreed to share their venison with us, and my wife and I agreed to share ours. When the hunt is over and one or the other of us has killed his deer, the fun begins. We have what is referred to as a "progressive dinner."

During these dinners, the lucky hunter provides the meat, while the other provides the charcoal grill and the side dishes. During the course of several weekends, we run through the gamut of meat dishes. We start off with charcoaled steaks, then we turn to roasts and ribs and finally end up with deerburgers. Before this ritual started, Jack and I were lovers of venison steaks, but our wives, however, could barely tolerate the thought of eating it. Today, it is the wife who keeps these gatherings going. We have charcoaled deer meat in snow, rain and wind. But we rarely miss a chance for one of these fine feasts. The wives not only like venison now, but they can hardly wait to get at it while it is cooking. Such progress in their eating habits is more than remarkable. This, alone, convinces me that anybody, no matter how finicky or fussy, who likes fine meat, will be delighted with a properly prepared charcoal venison steak or roast.

The process we use is relatively simple and a minimum of

trouble. However, on occasion we aim for complete culinary perfection and it does take longer. This is honest fun for us. It is a rare occasion, indeed, when we can afford such choice cuts of beef as we use of venison.

Charcoal cooking is not the only acceptable way to prepare those thick venison steaks, but it is the sure-fire way to indoctrinate the "beginner" with a type of venison "philosophy." In other words, you create the proper attitude toward venison in the future, by starting him off with the very best. Once tasted charcoaled, venison is thereafter held in high esteem, and the finicky eaters will surely become addicted to its natural goodness.

Cooking on the outside charcoal grill has grown in popularity with leaps and bounds in the past few years. When one combines that relatively new American pastime with the age-old pastime of hunting, he comes up with an eating delicacy that even the most finicky dieter cannot resist.

When one is about to indoctrinate a layman to the tempting barbecued venison steak, a few basics should be rounded up for the occasion. "Roughing" it, charcoal style, is part of the fun, but a certain amount of organization is in order. First off, one must have a sturdy portable grill that can be placed to suit the wind and weather of all types. A long handled fork, a knife, tongs and a basting brush are handy, as well as a scuttle and small shovel to handle the charcoal.

To speed the process up, Jack Wiley constructed a "blower" from a portable mixer motor and a model airplane propeller. This was used to fan the charcoal to a white heat in short order. It is much easier than blowing. Normally, charcoal is ready to cook steak over in around 30 minutes, but with the blower it takes only 10.

You have a number of favorite cuts of steak to choose from on a deer, just as you have on a cut of beef. Whether it be sirloin, club, boneless loin or a porterhouse, you are in for a treat. Our steak is usually cut about 1½ inches thick. Since deer are essentially lean animals, trimming the fat or other tissue can be left to the discretion of the cook. Making sure that the charcoal is within an inch or two from the grill, the edges should be scored every couple of inches and then laid flat on the grill.

From now on, we separate the "chefs" from the "housekeepers." The next few minutes can make or break our project. One should never leave the side of his "baby" once the meat is on the grill. Charcoal heat is fabulously hot, and a tender piece of deer meat can change without notice to a burned up mess.

While the meat is beginning to simmer, the lean side should be salted and peppered liberally, or according to taste. The other side will be treated exactly like this within a minute of its starting to cook. As quickly as salt and pepper are applied on the lean side, turn your steak and repeat on the partially seared side. Depending upon the thickness, in our case 1½ inches, steaks should be allowed to cook from 4 to 5 minutes for rare steak, then turn and cook the same time on the other side. If the outside of the steak pleases you, then you determine if it is just rare enough by observing the juices. When they begin to ooze out on top, your rare steak is ready. If you wish for rare to medium steak, allow each side to cook about four minutes longer.

An important point to keep in mind is that charcoal heat is so intense that a steak will often cook even when removed from the heat. They call this "exothermic" heat, and it penetrates the meat and remains intense even after the charcoal heat is removed externally.

Jack knew this from past experience with charcoaling beef, and he avoids the "build-up" of heat by literally walking it around the grill from time to time. Involved here is the simple process of grasping the steak in the middle or so that it won't tear, and taking a little walk around the grill. This takes perhaps 30 seconds, or even a minute, but you can tell when the steak quits cooking. Then place it back on the grill and cook to taste.

On occasion, we use a variety of sauces or mixtures to give some exotic flavor to our venison, but personally I prefer the salt and pepper treatment best. Actually, why people do it, I don't know, but it seems that nine out of ten cooks can't leave well enough alone. First off, they have an exotic type meat in venison, yet it is venison that normally gets the full treatment of sauces, oils and juices. Which means that what started off as a fine deer steak turns into an exotic, exotic deer steak. Thus, the true flavor is often missed in the process. Most experts seem to agree that basting meats with anything but olive oil or butter, or margarine, while cooking it toughens the meat.

Starting off with our steaks close to the heat serves a good purpose and should be followed without question. A quick heat tends to sear and seal in the natural juices of steaks. Otherwise, we would have constant dripping of these juices into the flame and at the same time our flavor and rareness would be lost.

Charcoal, itself, gives a particular personality to any meat. It imparts a particular color, taste and odor, none of which can fail to tempt the most finicky of diners. The heavenly odor of charcoaled deer steak makes one completely forget he is about to eat wild meat. But I don't say, and heaven forbid, that one should remove from steak its recognition as definitely venison. For venison is not beef, but it is as tender, juicy, and in my mind far more tasty than anything but the finest beef found on the market today. And when that fussy friend sits down to his first charcoaled venison steak, I predict without hesitation that he will admit he never tasted a better morsel.

When placed on the individual plates, surrounded by baked potatoes, coffee and a good green salad, every mouth will water for that first bite. If you choose, a touch of Worcestershire sauce can be added to the steak, or any particular fancy trimmings one desires. But wait until the meat has been properly cooked before bringing in your fancy garnishes. For experience's sake, try your venison first with nothing but the natural flavor, then add your garnishes a little at a time.

Once you have tried charcoaled steak, reach out for new fields to conquer. Try a sirloin roast of venison, one which is about as thick as it is wide. The ideal seems to be about 3 to 4 pounds. Allow it to assume room temperature after freezing or cold storage. Figure that this size chunk of deer meat will take about 15 minutes per roasting pound, if you like it rare; 20 to 25 minutes, if you like the meat medium done. In this case, you should rub salt and black pepper into the roast before charcoaling begins. Rub it into the meat until it will absorb no more. Turn the roast every 12 to 15 minutes to keep from charring and to keep cooking evenly throughout the meat.

Roast will assume a more heavily charred appearance than steak due to the longer time required to cook, but don't worry, a little bit helps the flavor. Roast, when done, should be placed on a smooth, solid base and then carved into thick chunks. It takes a minimum, usually, of about a pound of meat per person served — a lot? You bet, but watch it disappear.

Ways of preparing venison on the charcoal grill are about as versatile as the chef's imagination. Some of my favorites include kebabs, make up of one-inch squares of lean venison mingled with an assortment of vegetables, such as pepper, onions and tomatoes.

From all of these choice cuts of venison one normally has a certain amount of fairly lean scraps, which can be turned into excellent deerburgers. Mix one pound of tangy pork sausage, with one pound of venison, and have the butcher grind it all together. These burgers are a real charcoal treat for adults and children alike, and are treated just like any other hamburger.

Cutlets, meat loaf and fillets are some other fine venison treats over the charcoal grill, and by the next season we'll find more ways. Someday, I'd like to have a neighborhood feast of "pit charcoaled venison," using a half or whole deer. And then I'd like to invite every finicky friend I know to a barbecue feast. In one such venture, I'm thoroughly convinced that we could have one mass "conversion" from "fussy eaters" to "fanatic" lovers of deer meat, and surely somebody owes it to these people to show them what they are missing.

Homemade
Venison
Recipes

Kellybeckert

Grilling Venison

*It must be over 15 years ago now since I first had venison grilled outdoors on a homemade grill over a hardwood fire. No time for special seasonings, spices or fancy sauces to be used. There was hunting to be done. Maybe it was the hunting atmosphere that was behind it, but I can remember that venison was tender, and savory with just salt and pepper. Yes, savory, that is the best word to describe it. Later I learned...
the rest of the story.*

Why did the venison taste so good? It was because it was the quality cared for venison described earlier in our book. The deer was properly field dressed, cooled, aged, carefully processed, and double freezer wrapped. This made me see it does not take a fancy recipe to make quality venison taste good. It already is good and nutritious.

It is the goal of all the recipes in this GRILLING section, and the other sections as well, to give you great recipes that make your nutritious, quality venison taste even better for you and your family.

Read on for your grilling tips and great venison recipes — then go grill it on a gas grill, charcoal or water smoker...the recipes will all do a great job. Enjoy!

◘ Cooking Venison Using The Water Smoker

We have enjoyed eating venison prepared on our water smoker for over fifteen years now — so who knows how many delicious venison steaks, roasts, and burgers we have enjoyed.

Water Smoker Grilling Tips

● Venison should be thawed slowly in the refrigerator prior to cooking. A little additional aging does not hurt.

● Do not let water pan dry up. Coat drip pan with aluminum foil to help it retain water.

● Marinating venison helps break down the cellular structure, thus cooking time is reduced.

● If you are grilling or smoking one or more pieces of venison, the cooking time is based on the doneness of the largest piece.

● It is good to brush a venison roast that is smoked with melted butter seasoned with garlic powder, parsley, and onion powder prior to grilling.

Flavoring wood

Any fruit or nut tree wood chips can be used. Wood pieces 3 to 4 inches by 1 to 1½ inches thick smoke the best. Mesquite and hickory wood is excellent for venison.

Seasoning

Experiment with salt, herbs, spices and sauces on your quality cared for venison and it's always deliciously nutritious.

Basting

Not necessary for venison on a water smoker. Always check early for desired doneness. You may want to add water to the drip pan and marinade or venison sauce to the venison at the same time. An option to do that at check times would be to also add strips of bacon. It will add a nice flavor to venison while it finishes its cooking.

Go smoke up a storm!

◘ Venison Grilling Tips

Did you read the reprint in our book called "Venison Need Not Be 'Pot Luck' " on page 36? Those two hunters enjoy grilling nutritious venison as much as I do for my family and friends. Carefully handled venison from the start is a real treat when grilled as carefully as you would the best beef steak.

Venison barbecuing is simple if you are willing to take a few hints. It's simply not true that everyone knows how it is done.

Preparing lean venison is a breeze on the barbecue. A low fat cooking method like grilling (or broiling when you need to take a rain check) is an easy way to trim fat. Venison and lean meats stay lean because, unlike frying, grilling allows fat to drip away as meat cooks.

Try experimenting with rubs and marinades. Rubs are blends of dried herbs and spices that flavor the exterior of meat as it cooks. Marinades, made with herbs, spices, and an acidic liquid like wine vinegar or lemon juice, enhance the flavor of venison.

Adjust grilling temperature, either by allowing the coals to burn down before cooking or by moving the rack six inches or more away from the fire. Either method will slow down cooking sufficiently to allow the venison to brown gently while it firms through to its center.

Do not allow the fire to flame uncontrolled. Although some scorching is unavoidable when cooking over an open fire, it is never desirable, unless a blackening technique is being pursued. To ensure even brownness, turn venison frequently and move it away from flare-ups when they occur. It is helpful to keep a spray bottle of water by the grill to douse any flames.

Unfortunately timing directions for grilled venison can be only approximate. Because most grills do not have a thermostat, exact temperatures are impossible to control. Fires can flare up or die away without warning, so it is imperative to keep a close watch and check the venison regularly. It is more important that venison be properly browned, than it is for it to sit over the heat for the prescribed time stated in the recipe.

Happy grilling!

◘ Grilling Timetable Guide

The time required for grilling will vary depending on the type of barbecue equipment, temperature of the coals, and distance from the heat source. Here is a helpful time guide.

Venison Cuts

1 inch thick	**Time Each Side**
Rare	6 to 10 minutes
Medium	10 to 12 minutes
Well-done	12 to 18 minutes
1-1/2 inches thick	**Time Each Side**
Rare	8 to 12 minutes
Medium	12 to 16 minutes
Well-done	16 to 22 minutes
2 inches thick	**Time Each Side**
Rare	16 to 18 minutes
Medium	22 to 25 minutes
Well-done	35 to 45 minutes
2-1/2 - 3 inches thick	**Time Each Side**
Rare	18 to 25 minutes
Medium	30 to 40 minutes
Well-done	50 to 60 minutes

Venisonburger

60% venison/40% hamburger or ground pork*

Rare	8 to 10 minutes
Medium	12 to 13 minutes
Well-done	15 to 18 minutes

* When using ground pork, cook to well-done.

♨ Grilling Ground Venisonburgers

Add the following ingredients to One Pound Ground Venison:

All American Burgers

Liquid	Bread Grain	Vegetable Condiment	Seasoning	Bread Bun	Topping
1 Tbsp. mustard and 1 Tbsp. catsup	1/4 cup fine dry bread crumbs	1/3 cup finely chopped pickle	1/2 tsp. onion salt; dash pepper	Hamburger buns	Onion slices; tomato slices; lettuce leaves; pickle slices

Pizza Burgers

Liquid	Bread Grain	Vegetable Condiment	Seasoning	Bread Bun	Topping
2 Tbsp. pizza sauce	1/4 cup seasoned fine dry bread crumbs	1/3 cup chopped pitted ripe olives or chopped canned mushrooms	1/2 tsp. salt; 1/2 tsp. Italian seasoning	1 inch French bread slices	Warm 1/2 cup pizza sauce with 1/4 cup sliced pitted ripe olives. Spoon atop burgers. Top with mozzarella cheese slices

Salad Burgers

Liquid	Bread Grain	Vegetable Condiment	Seasoning	Bread Bun	Topping
2 Tbsp. creamy cucumber or ranch-style salad dressing	3 Tbsp. bulgar	1/3 cup chopped cucumber	1/2 tsp. garlic salt; 1/4 tsp. dried marjoram, crushed; dash pepper	Pita bread halves or kaiser bun	1/4 cup creamy cucumber or ranch-style salad dressing; alfalfa sprouts; cucumber and avocado slices

German Style Burgers

Liquid	Bread Grain	Vegetable Condiment	Seasoning	Bread Bun	Topping
2 Tbsp. beer	1/4 cup dry rye bread crumbs	1/4 cup shredded Muenster cheese	1/2 tsp. caraway seed; 1/2 tsp. salt; 1/4 tsp. pepper	Rye or Pumpernickel bread	Spread bread with mustard. Stir 1/4 tsp. caraway seed into 1/2 cup drained sauerkraut. Spoon atop burgers; top with Muenster cheese slices

Barbecued Venison Loin Steaks

3 to 4 pounds venison loin steak
1 (8 ounce) can tomato sauce
2 teaspoons salt
1/2 teaspoon black pepper
1/4 cup chili sauce
1/3 cup packed brown sugar
1/4 cup vinegar
2 tablespoons prepared mustard
1/2 cup chopped onion
4 cloves garlic, diced
1 tablespoon chili powder
1/2 teaspoon cayenne pepper

In a small saucepan, combine tomato sauce, salt, pepper, chili sauce, brown sugar, vinegar, mustard, onion, garlic, chili powder, and cayenne pepper. Bring to boiling over medium heat, stirring frequently. Reduce heat; simmer 5 minutes. Dip steaks in sauce, coating all sides. Grill over low heat 15 to 20 minutes or until done, turning and brushing with sauce occasionally.

Venison Hawaiian Marinated Kabobs

1/2 cup pineapple juice
2 tablespoons fresh lemon juice
1 small onion, finely chopped
2 tablespoons olive oil
1 clove garlic, minced
1/2 teaspoon salt
Dash freshly ground pepper
2 pounds cubed boneless venison steak
Quick cooking vegetables

Combine fruit juices, chopped onion, oil, garlic, salt, and pepper in glass, ceramic or stainless steel bowl. Add cubed venison. Cover and marinate in refrigerator 4 to 5 hours or overnight.

Preheat broiler. Drain meat, discarding marinade, and thread onto 6 skewers. Broil or grill about 4 inches from heat for 4 to 5 minutes. Remove venison from skewers then add venison, tomatoes, mushrooms, zucchini, onion or other quick cooking vegetables, alternating for variety. Finish barbecuing another 4 to 5 minutes to taste.

For a colorful variation on this recipe, broil the venison until nearly done, then add tomatoes, mushrooms, zucchini or other quick-cooking vegetables to skewers and finish cooking.

Memphis Grilled Venison Roast

Instant meat tenderizer (optional)
$\frac{1}{2}$ of a (5 ounce) bottle soy sauce
1 tablespoon lemon juice
1 teaspoon parsley
1 teaspoon thyme
2 to 3 pounds venison roast
$\frac{1}{4}$ cup packed brown sugar
$\frac{1}{4}$ cup bourbon or brandy
1 teaspoon Worcestershire sauce
$\frac{1}{2}$ cups water

Sprinkle meat tenderizer over roast following label directions. Place in a shallow pan or in a double plastic bag. In a small bowl, combine remaining ingredients; pour marinade over. Cover or seal. Refrigerate at least 6 hours, turning once. Drain marinade from roast; reserve marinade. Grill over hot coals 18 to 25 minutes or until desired doneness, turning and basting with marinade every 8 minutes or so.

Wine Marinated Venison Steak

2 pounds venison steaks 1 inch thick
Marinade:
$\frac{1}{2}$ cup red wine vinegar
$\frac{1}{2}$ cup water
1 medium onion, chopped
$1\frac{1}{2}$ teaspoons sugar
1 teaspoon salt
$\frac{1}{2}$ teaspoon crushed leaf basil
$\frac{1}{4}$ teaspoon celery seed
1 teaspoon thyme
1 teaspoon Italian seasoning
$\frac{1}{8}$ teaspoon black pepper

In a small saucepan, combine vinegar, water, onion, sugar, salt, basil, celery seed, thyme, Italian seasoning, and pepper; blend well. Simmer 10 minutes, stirring occasionally; cool. Place steak in a shallow pan or in a double plastic bag. Pour marinade over steak. Cover or seal. Refrigerate 6 to 8 hours or overnight, turning once. Drain marinade from steak; reserve marinade. Grill steak over hot coals until desired doneness, basting often. Do not overcook venison — it is best medium rare.

Nick's Zesty Venison Kabobs

1 pound venison round steak
1 cup oil and vinegar dressing
2 teaspoons Worcestershire
  sauce
1 teaspoon soy sauce
1 green pepper

1 (8 ounce) can small whole
  peeled boiled onions
1 (10 ounce) can unsweetened
  pineapple chunks (or any
  firm fresh or canned fruit)

For a hearty entree, cut venison in 1 inch cubes. Marinate meat in mixture of oil and vinegar dressing, Worcestershire sauce, and soy sauce for 12 to 24 hours in refrigerator. Prepare brochettes, alternating vegetables and pineapple chunks with meat on skewer, beginning with meat.

Place on coals approximately 4 to 6 inches from source of heat (the larger the cut, the greater the distance from the coals.) Cook on one side until brown; baste again with marinade sauce. Turn and cook on second side to desired doneness. One turning is all that's necessary. Delicious!

Sweet 'N Spicy BBQ Venison Steaks

1 pound venison loin steaks
Sweet n' spicy sauce:
1/2 cup prepared salsa or chili
  sauce
3 to 4 dashes Tabasco
1/4 cup water

1/2 cup ketchup
1/2 teaspoon garlic powder
2 tablespoons packed brown
  sugar
1 tablespoon Dijon-style
  mustard

In small bowl, combine sauce ingredients; mix well. Reserve 1/2 cup to serve as sauce. Place venison steaks on grid over ash-covered medium coals; grill 12 to 16 minutes for medium-rare to medium doneness, turning once. Brush both sides of steaks with remaining sauce during last 3 to 4 minutes of grilling. Carve steaks into slices; serve with reserved sauce. Makes 4 servings.

Venison Teriyaki

1 garlic clove, minced
1 tablespoon garlic powder
2 tablespoons salad oil
2 tablespoons soy sauce
¼ teaspoon Tabasco sauce
½ teaspoon dry mustard
1 bay leaf
½ lemon, thinly sliced
⅓ cup sherry or water

1 tablespoon Italian seasoning
2 tablespoons wine vinegar
2 teaspoons Worcestershire
   sauce
³/₄ teaspoon ginger
1 teaspoon salt
3 tablespoons sugar
2½ to 3 pounds boneless
   venison steaks

In a large shallow pan, combine all ingredients except meat. Mix well. Add steak; cover and refrigerate 6 hours or overnight, turning a few times.

Remove from refrigerator a half hour before cooking. If desired, pierce meat with fork and sprinkle with unseasoned tenderizer. Place on grill about 4 inches above prepared coals and broil about 10 minutes on each side or until desired doneness.

Grilled Venison Loin
With Seasoned Butter

¼ cup butter, melted
2 teaspoons lemon juice
4 tablespoons soy sauce
4 (16 ounce) venison loin steaks,
   cut lengthwise in half

1 teaspoon black pepper
1 teaspoon chili powder
1 teaspoon dried basil, crushed

Blend together melted butter, lemon juice, and soy sauce. Pour over steaks and marinate for 2 hours; then on waxed paper roll in pepper, chili powder and basil. Grill steaks over medium to hot coals 8 minutes on each side for medium-rare doneness. Serve hot off the grill — Do Not Overcook!

This "Venison Steak Grill" recipe was prepared one summer weekend for one of our female relatives who knew of my savory game cooking reputation. While enjoying her steak, she commented, "It is delicious. With venison steak this good and more nutritious than beef, I can now appreciate why you deer hunt."

Steve's Venison Steak Grill

1 (2 to 3 pound) venison round
    steak, cut 2 to 3 inches thick
½ cup cooking oil
½ cup dry red wine
2 tablespoons catsup
2 tablespoons molasses

2 tablespoons ginger
1 teaspoon prepared mustard
2 cloves garlic, minced
1½ teaspoons salt
5 to 6 drops hot sauce
½ teaspoon pepper

Poke the steak to help marinade penetration. Place in shallow baking dish. Combine cooking oil, wine, catsup, molasses, ginger, mustard, garlic, salt, hot sauce, and pepper. Pour over steak. Cover; let stand 3 hours at room temperature or 6 hours (or over-night) in refrigerator, turning several times.

Drain steak, reserving marinade and grill steak over medium coals for about 18 minutes on each side for rare, about 25 minutes on each side for medium-rare. Brush occasionally with reserved marinade.

Remove meat to serving platter. Carve across grain in thin slices. Try adding to steaks a parsley, mushroom, butter sauce. So good!

A DEER HUNTER'S WIFE KNOWS!
It took awhile but now Steve has, for some time, continued to listen to me. When he creates tasty dishes he has gotten into the habit of writing his ingredients and cooking process down for our neighbors, family and others to enjoy. These recipes are in all of our game cookbooks for you and yours to <u>enjoy</u>...Many are better than "restaurant quality."

The "Steak with Country Sauce" recipe has been a family favorite on the grill for the last eight years. It is special! Try it with your venison and see if you do not agree!

Steak With Country Sauce

2 pounds venison steaks
1 teaspoon garlic salt
½ teaspoon black pepper
2 slices bacon, diced
1 medium onion, chopped

½ cup grape jelly
4 to 5 drops Tabasco sauce
1 tablespoon cider vinegar
½ cup catsup or chili sauce

Sprinkle garlic salt and pepper on both sides of steak. Place steak in a shallow pan or double plastic bag; set aside. In a large skillet, fry bacon until crisp; push to one side. Add onion; saute until onion is golden. Add remaining ingredients; simmer until jelly melts and mixture is smooth, stirring occasionally. Pour sauce over steak. Cover or seal. Let stand 2 hours, turning steak once. Drain sauce from steak. Grill 8 to 10 minutes a side or until desired doneness, brushing several times with sauce. Heat remaining sauce and serve with sliced steak. Add baked beans and fresh corn on the cob — makes for a delicious meal.

Family Style
Grilled Venison Steaks

2 pounds venison steaks
3 tablespoons steak sauce
½ cup red wine vinegar
½ cup red cooking wine
½ cup chopped onion
5 to 6 drops Tabasco sauce

1 cup bottled barbecue sauce, or
   make your own
2 tablespoons Dijon mustard
1 teaspoon chili powder
1 teaspoon salt
1 teaspoon pepper

Combine all ingredients except steak in blender for marinade. In plastic bag, marinate steaks in marinade several hours or overnight. Drain. Grill steaks 5 to 7 minutes on each side or until cooked as desired. Suggest basting steaks with marinade while grilling.

Chuckwagon Steak

About 1 pound venison hind
   quarter steak
1 clove garlic, diced
1 (15 ounce) can tomato sauce
   or chili sauce
¼ cup vegetable oil

1 small onion, chopped
2 tablespoons red wine vinegar
1 teaspoon brown sugar
1 teaspoon crushed red pepper
   flakes

Score both sides of steak with a sharp knife. In a small bowl, combine garlic, tomato sauce, oil, onion, vinegar, brown sugar, and red pepper flakes; blend well. Place steak in a shallow pan or in a marinade dish. Pour sauce over steak and cover. Refrigerate at least 3 hours. Drain sauce from steak; reserve sauce. Grill over hot coals until desired doneness, turning and basting after 8 minutes. To serve, cut crosswise into thin slices. Heat remaining sauce and serve with steak.

Italian Style Venisonburgers

1½ pounds ground venison
1 egg; lightly beaten
1¼ teaspoons salt
1 cup soft bread crumbs
2 tablespoons grated Parmesan
  cheese

1½ teaspoons Italian seasoning
1 (4 ounce) can mushrooms
  (pieces and stems), drained
Sliced Italian bread (optional)

In a small bowl, combine all ingredients, except mushrooms and bread; blend well. Shape into 6 to 8 burgers. Grill over hot coals 6 to 10 minutes each side. Serve on sliced Italian bread, topped with mushrooms and a slice of cheese, if desired.

Stuffing Stuffed Venisonburgers

1½ pounds venisonburger or
  venison sausage
1½ teaspoons salt
1 cup seasoned stuffing mix
¼ cup butter or margarine

¼ teaspoon black pepper
1 medium onion, grated
2 tablespoons lemon juice
Dash cayenne pepper
6 slices Velveeta or Swiss cheese

In a medium bowl, combine venison and salt; blend well. In a small bowl, combine remaining ingredients except cheese; blend well into venison. Now divide into 12 equal portions. Flatten each portion between pieces of waxed paper into 5-inch patties. Do not remove patties from waxed paper. Divide stuffing mixture among 6 of the patties. Top each with a second patty; press edges together to seal. Remove from waxed paper. Grill over medium-hot coals until desired doneness. Add slices of Swiss or Velveeta cheese to burgers. Great!

Herb And Wine
Barbecued Deer Roast

3 pound venison roast
½ cup olive oil
1 tablespoon crushed leaf
    marjoram
1 teaspoon minced garlic
5 to 6 drops Tabasco sauce

2 cups dry red wine
2 tablespoons instant minced
    onion
1 tablespoon salt
¼ teaspoon black pepper
1 tablespoon parsley

Place roast in a shallow pan or in a double plastic bag. In a small bowl, combine remaining ingredients; pour over meat. Cover or seal. Refrigerate about 24 hours, turning 2 or 3 times. Drain marinade from roast; reserve marinade. Grill over hot coals 18 to 25 minutes or until desired doneness, turning and basting with marinade every 6 minutes or so.

Mustard Buttered
Venison Steaks

2 tablespoons butter, softened
2 tablespoons prepared
    mustard
1 teaspoon Italian seasoning

1 teaspoon garlic powder
4 venison steaks, about 1½ inch
    thick

In a small dish, blend butter and mustard, Italian seasoning, and garlic powder; set aside. Grill over medium-hot coals 4 to 5 minutes on each side. Spread mustard butter over steak; grill 1 to 2 minutes. Turn steaks and spread the other side with mustard butter. Grill until desired doneness.

Picnic Venison Steak

2 to 3 pounds venison steaks,
1½ inches thick
2 cups burgundy wine
2 tablespoons Worcestershire
sauce

1 teaspoon onion powder
¼ teaspoon black pepper
¼ teaspoon garlic powder

Place steak in a shallow pan or in a double plastic bag. Pour wine and Worcestershire sauce over steak; sprinkle on seasonings. Cover or seal. Refrigerate overnight, turning once. Next day drain marinade from steak; reserve marinade. Grill over medium hot coals until desired doneness, basting occasionally with marinade.

Teriyaki Steak Sandwiches

2 to 3 pounds venison steaks
½ cup soy sauce
½ cup olive oil

2 tablespoons chopped onion
1 clove garlic, diced
2 tablespoons brown sugar

In a large, flat baking dish or plastic container, combine soy sauce, olive oil, onion, garlic, and brown sugar; stir to dissolve sugar. Add steaks to marinade; turn to coat well. Refrigerate at least 3 hours. Drain marinade from steaks; reserve marinade. Grill steaks over hot coals 4 to 6 minutes on each side. Venison is best cooked medium rare, pink in the middle. Cut into pieces and serve on sliced hard rolls. Add your favorite potato salad and enjoy!

Grilled Venison Rosé

3 cloves garlic, minced
3 tablespoons olive oil
½ cup rosé wine
2 tablespoons lemon juice
1 teaspoon dried basil, crushed
1 teaspoon dry mustard
1 teaspoon salt

2 tablespoons bottled steak
   sauce
2 tablespoons Worcestershire
   sauce
2½ to 3 pounds venison roast,
   cut 1½ inches thick round
   steaks

In a small bowl, combine garlic, oil, wine, lemon juice, basil, dry mustard, and salt. Prick roast on both sides with a long-tined fork; place in plastic bag and set in deep bowl. Marinate overnight in refrigerator, turning roast in bag or pressing marinade against roast occasionally. Drain meat, reserving marinade. Add steak sauce and Worcestershire sauce to reserved marinade. Remove excess moisture from roast with paper toweling. Grill over medium-hot coals 25 to 30 minutes on each side for medium doneness, brushing with marinade. Turn roast with tongs once it is seared all over to retain its juices. Do not overcook or catsup/steak sauce will be needed.

Hawaiian Venison Kabobs

½ cup soy sauce
¼ cup olive oil
1 tablespoon dark corn syrup
2 cloves garlic, mined
1 teaspoon prepared mustard
1 teaspoon onion powder
1 teaspoon ground ginger

2½ pounds venison steak, cut
   into 1½ inch pieces
3 green peppers, cut into 1 inch
   squares
5 small firm tomatoes,
   quartered

In large bowl combine soy sauce, oil, corn syrup, garlic, prepared mustard, onion powder, and ginger. Add meat; cover and refrigerate several hours or overnight. Drain meat, reserving marinade. Alternate meat, green pepper and tomato on skewers. Grill over medium-hot coals till desired doneness; Allow about 15 minutes for medium-rare. Baste the kabobs occasionally with reserved marinade. Be careful not to overcook. Enjoy!

Pizza Patties

1 pound ground venison or
    venisonburger
¾ cup cracker crumbs
1 small onion, minced
¼ teaspoon crushed leaf
    oregano
1 egg, lightly beaten

¼ cup red wine
½ cup grated mozzarella cheese
1 clove garlic, minced
Salt and pepper to taste
¼ cup tomato paste or chili
    sauce
4 hamburger or hoagie rolls

In a large bowl, combine all ingredients, except rolls; blend well. Shape into 4 patties. Grill over hot coals until desired doneness.

Marinated Deer Kabobs

2 pounds venison steak, cut into
    1 inch cubes
¼ cup olive oil
2 tablespoons cider vinegar
½ teaspoon salt
1 teaspoon celery salt
1 teaspoon onion salt
¾ teaspoon garlic salt

¾ teaspoon crushed leaf
    oregano
½ teaspoon pepper
6 medium mushroom caps
1 small summer squash,
    cut in ½ inch pieces
1 small zucchini, cut in ½ inch
    pieces

In a small saucepan, combine oil, vinegar, all salts, oregano, and pepper. Bring to boiling; remove from heat; let stand until cool. Place meat in a shallow pan or in a double plastic bag. Add mushrooms, squash, and zucchini. Pour marinade over meat and vegetables. Cover or seal. Refrigerate 4 to 6 hours, turning occasionally. Alternately thread meat and vegetables on 6 skewers. Grill over hot coals 8 to 10 minutes or until desired doneness, basting often with marinade. Some kind of good!

Ah, yes, "Wined and Dined Venison Roast."
We remember it well because we have one
venison sirloin tip roast each year for grilling
with this favorite recipe. Enjoy!

Wined And Dined
Venison Roast

1 (3 pound) venison roast,
    cut 2 to 3 inches thick
3 cloves garlic, minced
3 tablespoons cooking oil
½ cup dry red wine
2 tablespoons lemon juice

1 teaspoon dried basil, crushed
1 tablespoon prepared mustard
1 teaspoon garlic salt
2 tablespoons bottled steak
    sauce

Cook garlic in oil; remove from heat. Add wine, lemon juice, basil, mustard, and 1 teaspoon garlic salt. Prick roast on both sides with long-tined fork; place in plastic bag and set in deep bowl. Pour in wine mixture; close bag. Marinate overnight in refrigerator, turning roast in bag or pressing marinade against roast occasionally. Drain meat, reserving marinade. Remove excess moisture from roast with paper toweling. Add steak sauce to reserved marinade. Grill roast over medium coals 25 to 30 minutes on each side for medium doneness. Brush with marinade.

Optional: Slice marinated venison roast before grilling. Grill 8 to 10 minutes per side. Watch your fire so as to not overcook!

Teriyaki Venisonburger Steak

2 pounds venison or
   venisonburger
3 teaspoons salt
1 teaspoon onion powder
¼ teaspoon black pepper
2 tablespoons minced parsley

Bottled teriyaki sauce
1 teaspoon garlic powder
6 green onions, sliced
   diagonally
8 hamburger rolls

In a large bowl, combine ground venison, salt, onion powder, pepper, parsley, 2 tablespoons teriyaki sauce and garlic powder; mix lightly. Shape into 8 to 1¼ inch thick oval patties. Brush on teriyaki sauce. Grill over medium hot coals until desired doneness, brushing occasionally with teriyaki sauce. Carefully remove burgers from grill with two spatulas. Serve on hamburger rolls topped with sliced green onions.

Black Olive Venison Steak

2½ to 3 pound venison steak
   (about 1½ inches thick)
1 cup sliced black olives
2 cloves garlic, diced

⅓ cup lemon juice
3 tablespoons olive oil
Instant meat tenderizer
   (optional)

Place steak in a shallow pan or in a double plastic bag. Top with olives. In a small bowl, combine garlic, lemon juice, and oil; pour over steak. Cover or seal. Refrigerate at least 8 hours, turning steak once. Drain marinade from steak; reserve marinade. Sprinkle on meat tenderizer following label directions. Grill about 4 inches from medium-hot coals 8 to 12 minutes on each side or until desired doneness. Venison is best rare to medium rare.

Company's Coming Venison Roast

1 cup catsup
¼ cup cooking oil
¼ cup wine vinegar
2 tablespoons minced dried onion
2 tablespoons Worcestershire sauce
1 tablespoon brown sugar
1 teaspoon mustard seed

1 teaspoon dried oregano, crushed
1 bay leaf
1 teaspoon garlic salt
1 teaspoon salt
½ teaspoon pepper
1 teaspoon chili powder
½ cup water
1 (3 to 4 pound) boneless venison roast sliced in half

In sauce pan combine catsup, cooking oil, wine vinegar, onion, Worcestershire sauce, brown sugar, mustard seed, oregano, bay leaf, garlic salt, salt, pepper, chili powder and ½ cup water. Simmer the mixture 20 minutes; then remove the bay leaf. Pour sauce over the venison in container to marinate over night. Grill the roast cut into steaks on your favorite grill using left over sauce for basting. Grill steaks 8 to 10 minutes each side.

 Grilling Tip:

Venison is great medium rare to medium. Most tender and juicy too!! Do not overcook because venison is very lean meat that does not need to be well done to taste great. Overcooking drys the venison out so it gets tougher the more you grill it.

A DEER HUNTER'S WIFE KNOWS!

If your family is not doing it already it is time to get started. Here is a very useful suggestion or tip. After your Labor Day venison barbecue with family and friends, it is time to start preparing your freezer for fresh game of all kinds or it may be just nutritious venison.

Your frozen double wrapped venison is now nine to ten months old. Time to pull out our Quality Venison cookbooks and prepare some ahead of time tasty, nutritious, venison meals for family, friends or even the soup kitchen in your town or church who serves the needy in your area. Venison from the whitetail deer is a gift from God and should never be wasted...

Prepare last year's venison or game now ahead of time and freeze the meals for later easy meals when you need them in October, November, December, when it's time to hunt or be with family. The frozen dishes will keep for another year if need be. You will be glad you did because later when eaten they will taste as good as when you first prepared them.

The "Tar Heal Rubbed Venison Steak" recipe is another family grilling recipe along with "Grilled Venison Rose." We like the Tar Heal flavor of the dry rub and we keep the spices in a covered container for numerous grilling uses all through the summer. This recipe uses a spicy dry rub to coat your choice of venison for grilling. While grilling, baste venison steaks or roast pieces with some of dry rub after adding enough vinegar to make a sauce.

Tar Heal Rubbed Venison Steak Or Roasts

Venison of your choice
Dry Rub Ingredients:
¼ cup sugar
¼ cup paprika
¼ cup chili powder

¼ cup black pepper
2 tablespoons onion powder
2 tablespoons garlic powder
1 tablespoon salt
Vinegar, for basting

Mix all ingredients in a small bowl. Coat the venison with dry rub spices by pressing it into the meat by hand; preparing it for grilling. Put some rub in a cup and add enough vinegar for basting your venison. Save remaining rub in a covered container for other barbecues.

Grill venison over medium to hot coals 8 to 10 minutes per side and do not overcook. Venison is best medium rare to medium doneness.

Grilled Oriental Venison Steaks

1½ to 2 pounds venison steaks,
   1 inch thick
1 cup sugar
1 cup water
1 cup soy sauce

½ teaspoon ground ginger
½ teaspoon garlic salt or 1 clove
   garlic, diced
1 tablespoon Accent spice

Heat and blend sugar and water together, then add other ingredients except Accent. Sprinkle Accent generously on steaks. Pour liquid mixture over steaks in covered marinator, (any covered container) and marinate 24 hours. Charcoal grill on medium to low heat turning every 10 minutes and basting with marinade sauce occasionally. Grill to medium rare. Delicious!

Grilled Marinated Leg Of Venison For Holiday Picnic

1 (7 to 9 pound) leg quarter of venison, boned and closely trimmed, butterflied (open) muscles separated into 3 to 4 large pieces
2 teaspoons salt
1 teaspoon black pepper
1 cup green onions, chopped
1 tablespoon parsley
1⅓ cups olive oil
½ cup vinegar or lemon juice
½ cup rose wine
2½ tablespoons rosemary
4 cloves garlic, sliced

Bone and butterfly venison if not done already. Do not slice through venison but trim and separate muscles. Place in large glass dish or stainless pan to marinate.

In a small bowl, combine salt, pepper, onions, parsley, olive oil, vinegar, wine and rosemary. Pour marinade mixture over venison and place the garlic slivers on the venison. Marinate at room temperature for 3 hours, or 6 to 8 hours in the refrigerator, turning occasionally.

Prepare your charcoal fire. Grill venison when coals are 'white hot' or grey in color. Grill by turning with a tong and baste with marinade until desired doneness, or about 45 to 60 minutes. Venison steak is best, juicy, medium to medium rare.

🔥 Grilling Tip:

With slight adjustments this venison recipe can be done in a water smoker. Roast 4 to 5 hours or when meat thermometer reaches 160 degrees (medium done). Be careful not to overcook. Covering your venison leg quarter with bacon strips while smoking over hickory or mesquite chips will keep the venison moist and flavorful.

Over one of the important holidays over the summer, we will prepare the "Picnic Venison Hind Quarter" recipe. If we do not have a hind quarter saved, we ad lib and halve the recipe. We will use one or two hind quarter roasts to come up with four or five pounds of venison and use just half of the recipe ingredients. The venison turns out just delicious!

Picnic Venison Hind Quarter
On Your Water Smoker

6 to 8 pounds venison roast or roasts, marinated in Dutch oven 12 hours or over night before smoking
8 ounces Rose wine
3 ounces olive oil
2 ounces Worcestershire sauce
2 tablespoons spicy mustard
4 ounces soy sauce
2 ounces lime juice
8 ounces tomato juice
2 teaspoons black pepper

First, before smoking, brown venison in your oven for 45 minutes at 400 degrees to sear in juices. Then smoke with hickory or mesquite chips 3 to 4 hours to catch venison medium to medium rare for its best flavor.

I recommend venison being boned and fat trimmed before freezing this valuable meat and certainly before grilling. Can use leftover marinade one last time to pour over roast for extra flavor before it drains into water pan.

Optional: 6 to 8 pounds of substitute beef or lamb can be used. Also will be delicious — Ah!

This "Garlic Marinated Venison Steak" recipe, whether cooked in your broiler or on your grill, will delight your taste buds. Give it a try and see.

Garlic Marinated Venison Steak

1½ to 2 pounds venison steak
2 teaspoons spicy mustard
   (your choice)
⅓ cup red wine vinegar
1 teaspoon salt

4 large garlic cloves, peeled and
   flattened or diced
1 cup olive oil
½ teaspoon black pepper

Peel all garlic and flatten by pressing down with wide blade of a knife. Place it in a jar with a tight fitting lid. Add remaining ingredients, except steak. Secure the lid and shake.

Poke the venison steak with a knife and place in a plastic bag with ½ marinade. Save ½ marinade for basting. Let it marinate for from 30 minutes to hours, depending on the cut of venison. It's your call.

Broil steak 3 inches from heat for 3 minutes on each side or until done to your taste. (Steak should not be cooked more than medium rare, since it is very lean meat and gets tough if over cooked.)

Optional: After marinating venison steaks grill it over charcoal 8 to 10 minutes a side. Baste with reserved fresh marinade to your desired doneness. Be careful not to over cook.

Mushroom Bacon Burgers

2 pounds ground venison or venisonburger
1 (8 ounce) can mushroom stems and pieces, drained
1/4 cup minced onion
1 teaspoon salt or seasoned salt
1 teaspoon black pepper
8 slices bacon, crisp-cooked and crumbled
Butter sauce (optional, recipe follows)
8 hamburger rolls, split

In a large bowl, combine ground venison, mushrooms, onion, seasonings and bacon; blend well. Shape mixture into 8 patties. Chill 1 hour. Grill over medium-hot coals 12 to 13 minutes or until desired doneness, brushing often with butter sauce, if desired.

Butter Sauce

1/2 cup butter
1/2 cup chopped onion
1/2 cup catsup
1/4 cup packed brown sugar
1/2 teaspoons chili powder
1 teaspoon garlic powder
1 teaspoon salt
1/8 teaspoon black pepper
3 tablespoons Worcestershire sauce
Dash hot pepper sauce

In a small saucepan, melt butter. Saute onion until tender. Stir in catsup, brown sugar, chili powder, garlic powder, salt, pepper, Worcestershire and hot pepper sauce. Simmer 5 minutes, stirring often. Makes 1 cup. This sauce is tasty and can be used on all your venison steak whether grilled or oven broiled.

When your family or friends are having a large picnic, you owe it to yourself to try this "Barbecue Hind Quarter of Venison" recipe. If blessed with an ample amount of venison, try to save a hind quarter after boning or quartering a deer especially for this recipe. It is worth it — enjoy!

Barbecued Hind Quarter Of Venison
Using Water Smoker

1 hind quarter of venison, thawed and boned a day or two before your picnic (if not done already)
1 pound bacon, Important!
Sauce: (Make the night before)
1/2 cup melted butter
1 cup cider vinegar
1 cup chili sauce
1/4 cup prepared mustard
1/4 cup Worcestershire sauce

1/4 cup burgundy wine
3 tablespoons chili powder
3 teaspoons pepper
1/2 cup olive oil
1 cup red wine vinegar
1/2 cup sugar
2 large onions, chopped
1/4 cup lemon juice
2 tablespoons dry mustard
3 teaspoons salt
3 cloves garlic, diced

Make sauce by combining above ingredients in a pan and bring to a simmer for 10 minutes. Pour sauce over boned hind quarter of venison in a large pan and poke holes in the meat to allow sauce to marinade the venison overnight.

Next morning turn venison over to marinade other side thoroughly for 3 or 4 more hours.

You will use the bacon to moisten the lean venison as it smokes and roasts for approximately 5 to 6 hours. Start your charcoal or water smoker after filling drip pan with water and adding moistened apple, mesquite or hickory wood chips to your heating method.

Coat your venison quarter completely with barbecue sauce and place on grill. Pour some sauce on top and layer with half of bacon. After three hours remove bacon, turn venison over. Add sauce to coat and new remaining bacon to the new up side of the venison. Check if done after 5 hours. Since venison is best medium rare to medium, be careful not to overcook.

Slice venison and use up any remaining barbecue sauce over steaks. Some work, yes, but delicious and surely worth all your effort. Enjoy! Guaranteed delicious.

Over the Labor Day weekend we got together with Mark and Jim's family for a picnic. We deer hunt together and since I am the 'cook' and I had some venison that I could prepare, they asked me to bring it along. The "Howland's Island Venison Steaks" recipe truly had everyone delighted and asking, "Steve, how did you do that?" Enjoyed medium rare it was truly memorable venison steak.

Howland's Island Venison Steaks

2 pounds venison loin steak,
   sliced lengthwise in half
   (about 1½ inches thick)
¼ cup olive oil
2 garlic cloves, diced
¼ cup Worcestershire sauce

½ teaspoon liquid smoke
   (optional)
¼ cup red wine, your choice
¾ cup soy sauce
1 teaspoon black pepper

Combine all ingredients except steaks. Then marinate your steaks 2 to 4 hours. Liquid smoke would give your venison steaks extra smoky flavor. Excellent idea if steaks are broiled in oven. Drain steaks and sear in juices by cooking one minute with grill in lowest grill position. Do same searing to other side. Then raise grill and cook 8 to 10 minutes each side medium rare to medium doneness, basting venison occasionally to keep it moist and tender. As always, enjoy!

Hawaiian Venison Burgers

2 pounds ground venison or
    venisonburger
½ cup minced onion
2 teaspoons salt
¼ teaspoon black pepper
2 eggs

3 tablespoons prepared
    mustard
3 tablespoons catsup
2 tablespoons soy sauce
8 pineapple slices, drained and
    heated
8 slices Swiss or cheddar cheese

In a large bowl, combine ground venison, onion, salt, pepper, and eggs; blend well. Shape into 8 large patties; set aside. In a small bowl, combine mustard, catsup, and soy sauce; blend well. Brush mustard mixture over burgers. Grill over low heat until desired doneness. Serve each topped with a pineapple slice and a slice of Swiss or cheddar cheese.

Cooking Venison Italian Style

We are always delighted and occasionally surprised how rich tasting Italian-style recipes turn out when venison is used instead of beef or even pork. Properly aged and frozen venison adds a savory flavor to pasta sauces and chili. Venison lasagna is a flavorful dish that is very hard to beat, for example. Quality venison makes all your meals taste better and it's more nutritious for you, too!

Try this "Italian Style Venison Sausage" recipe as soon as you can. It makes four pounds of fresh sausage but you will want to freeze only three and use one pound in the "Four Cheese Pasta with Venison" recipe or others in this Italian Cooking Section. It is good!

Italian Style Venison Sausage

3 pounds ground venison
1 pound ground pork
2 cloves garlic, minced
2 teaspoons fennel seeds
1 tablespoon salt
1 tablespoon parsley

½ teaspoon fresh ground pepper
1 teaspoon finely chopped or
   crushed red chili peppers
1 tablespoon Italian seasoning
2 to 3 teaspoons cayenne pepper
   (optional for hot sausage)

First grind 3 pounds venison or add it from butcher to 1 pound ground pork from your grocer. Mince garlic and blend with salt and fennel seeds. Add to meat and blend by hand. Then add parsley, black and red peppers and Italian seasoning. Mix thoroughly again. If you want hot sausage, mix in cayenne pepper to taste!

Roll into 4 one pound balls or loaves and place on freezer paper. Try one ball fresh. Wrap other 3 one pound balls of sausage in plastic freezer wrap and drop into one quart size freezer bags for quality freezer protection. Lean and tasty, enjoy!

Four Cheese Pasta With Venison

8 ounce penne or other tube
   pasta
1 pound ground venison
1 (14½ ounce) can stewed
   tomatoes
1 (8 ounce) can tomato sauce
1 teaspoon garlic powder

1 cup sliced green onions
1 (3 ounce) package cream cheese
½ cup shredded Parmesan cheese
½ cup shredded Swiss cheese
½ cup shredded sharp Cheddar
   cheese or cheese of your choice

Cook pasta as package directs; drain. In skillet, brown venison. Salt and pepper to taste. Add tomatoes, tomato sauce, garlic powder and cook uncovered, until slightly thickened. Stir in onions and cream cheese. Toss with remaining ingredients. Cover 5 minutes to melt cheeses and serve sauce over pasta. Garlic bread, please!

Steubenville Venison Pasta

1 pound ground venisonburger
Olive oil for browning as needed
1 cup shredded carrots
2/3 cup chopped onion
1 clove garlic, crushed
1 teaspoon basil leaves, crushed
1 teaspoon oregano, crushed

1 beef bouillon cube
1 teaspoon sugar
1/2 teaspoon Italian Seasoning
2 (15 ounce) cans tomato sauce
4 to 6 fresh mushrooms, sliced
1 pound package pasta

In a large skillet, brown venison in olive oil until it loses redness. Add carrots, onion and garlic. Saute until onion is tender. Add remaining ingredients except spaghetti. Cover, simmer 20 minutes. Stir occasionally. Prepare pasta according to package directions. Drain. Serve sauce over hot cooked pasta. An easily delicious pasta recipe, give it a try!

Venison Spaghetti Sauce Italiano

1 pound bulk venison sausage
1/2 cup chopped onion
2 cloves garlic, minced
1 (16 ounce) can whole
    tomatoes, cut up
1 (8 ounce) can tomato sauce
8 ounces fresh mushrooms,
    sliced
1/2 cup chopped green sweet
    pepper

2 tablespoons spicy mustard
1 bay leaf
1 teaspoon dried Italian
    seasoning, crushed
1/4 teaspoon black pepper
1/4 teaspoon red pepper
1/2 teaspoon salt
1 cup water

In a skillet cook sausage, onion, and garlic till meat is brown and onion is tender.

Meanwhile, in a 3½ or 4 quart crock pot combine undrained tomatoes, tomato sauce, mushrooms, green sweet pepper, mustard, bay leaf, Italian seasoning, black and red pepper, and salt. Stir in meat mixture and add 1 cup water; stir.

Cover; cook on low heat setting for 8 to 10 hours or on high heat setting for 4 to 5 hours. Discard bay leaf. Serve over 1 pound cooked pasta with favorite Italian or garlic bread!

Pasta With Savory Venison Tomatoes

1 pound ground venison,
    burger or sausage
1 cup chopped onion
2 cloves garlic, minced
¼ cup olive oil
3½ cups (29 ounce can) tomato
    puree
1¾ cups (14½ ounce can)
    stewed tomatoes
1 (6 ounce) can tomato paste

1½ tablespoons salt
2 teaspoons sugar
1 teaspoon oregano
1 teaspoon Italian seasoning
½ teaspoon black pepper
2 tablespoons chopped parsley
1 cup water
1 pound pasta of your choice
Parmesan cheese

In 5 quart Dutch oven saute venison with onion and garlic in oil until browned. Stir in remaining ingredients except pasta and Parmesan cheese. Bring to a boil. Reduce heat; cover and simmer 2 hours. Cook pasta according to package directions; drain. Serve sauce over hot cooked pasta; sprinkle with Parmesan cheese

Italian Style Venison Roast

1½ to 2 pounds venison roast
    chunks
3 medium-size onions, chopped
2 small tomatoes, chopped
4 carrots, sliced
4 stalks of celery, chopped
1 teaspoon parsley
1 teaspoon oregano

1 teaspoon salt, or to taste
1 teaspoon Italian seasoning
2 bay leaves
1 teaspoon black pepper
½ cup dry red wine
½ cup water
½ pound hot Italian sausage,
    sliced

Trim carefully and remove all surplus fibers, skin, and fat from venison roast, and cut into chunks. Place the chopped and sliced vegetables and seasonings in a slow cooker with equal parts of red wine and water. Add the venison and cover with sausage; cover the cooker and simmer on low heat 4 to 5 hours. Remove venison and sausage to a serving dish. Pour the slow cooker liquid and veggies over the sausage and roast chunks, and serve over noodles or rice, Ah!

Oh, so you are in the mood for Italian food either tonight or tomorrow night. "Steve's Venison Meatballs and Zippy Pasta Sauce" is the answer to a nutritious Italian meal. You can make half the recipe and stop it after the meatballs are baked if dinner is not until tomorrow night after all, or complete the recipe and feed five or six. That's Italian!

Steve's Venison Meatballs And Zippy Pasta Sauce

½ cup water
6 slices bread, torn in small pieces
1 pound ground venison or sausage
½ pound ground pork
1 teaspoon garlic powder
½ teaspoon hot pepper flakes
½ cup chopped onions

½ cup grated Romano cheese
2 eggs slightly beaten
2 teaspoons olive oil
½ teaspoon black pepper
½ teaspoon minced garlic
1 pound hot cooked pasta
2 (27 to 30 ounce) jars of favorite pasta sauce

In a small bowl pour water over bread; let soak 5 minutes. In large bowl, mix soaked bread with remaining ingredients (except pasta and pasta sauce). Shape meat into 15 to 16 oversized balls. Place meatballs in 2x9x13 inch baking pan. Bake uncovered, at 350 degrees for 30 minutes; drain, if needed. Pour pasta sauce over meatballs and bake 20 minutes longer. Serve over hot cooked pasta of your choice. Hope you all are really hungry. Enjoy!

A DEER HUNTER'S WIFE KNOWS!
Antlers are not important. They are not nutritious and inedible in any recipe, even in ours. With us deer hunting has never been about the size of the buck's horns. It has been about deer hunting to provide nutritiously delicious venison to enjoy with family, relatives, and friends and often with the needy in our local community.

Spicy Venison Spaghetti

1 pound ground venisonburger
½ pound ground pork
1 medium onion, chopped
2 tablespoons dry bread crumbs
¼ cup chopped fresh parsley
¼ cup milk
1 teaspoon seasoned salt
¼ teaspoon pepper
1 tablespoon olive oil
1 (28 ounce) can whole
    tomatoes, cut up, undrained
1 (6 ounce) can tomato paste

1 bay leaf
½ teaspoon salt
½ teaspoon sugar
½ teaspoon fennel seed,
    crushed
½ teaspoon basil leaves
⅛ teaspoon oregano
⅛ teaspoon crushed red pepper
1 pound package spaghetti,
    uncooked
¼ to ½ cup grated Parmesan
    cheese

In medium bowl, combine first eight ingredients; mix well. In Dutch oven, brown meat mixture in olive oil. Add remaining ingredients, except spaghetti and Parmesan cheese.

Bring to boil. Reduce heat; simmer, covered at least one hour, stirring occasionally. Prepare spaghetti according to package directions; drain. Serve with spicy venison sauce. Top with Parmesan cheese. Now that tastes Italian!

Low Fat Venison Pasta Sauce

1 pound ground venisonburger
    or cubes
½ pound ground pork or
    sausage
2 tablespoons olive oil
1 cup sliced mushrooms
½ cup chopped onions
½ cup chopped celery
½ cup chopped green pepper
3 garlic cloves, diced
2 tablespoons parsley

1 (6 ounce) can tomato paste
2 teaspoons salt
½ teaspoon oregano
½ teaspoon crushed red pepper
1 bay leaf
1 (28 ounce) can tomatoes
1 (8 ounce) can tomato sauce
1½ teaspoons basil
¼ teaspoon paprika
½ teaspoon black pepper
½ teaspoon chili powder

In a 3 quart Dutch oven brown venisonburger or cubes and pork in olive oil 10 to 15 minutes. Add mushrooms, onion, celery, green pepper and garlic and saute 10 to 15 minutes, stirring several times. Then add parsley and remaining ingredients. Simmer venison pasta sauce 2 hours or longer, checking to stir or add more water for desired thickness.

My wife Gale's recipe, "Gale's Spicy Venison Pasta," has been a favorite of ours for years. With quality cared for venison or sausage, it is a delicious Italian dish. Try it for yourself and you will be glad you did.

Gale's Spicy Venison Pasta

1 pound ground venisonburger
   or sausage
1 medium onion, chopped
2 tablespoons dry bread crumbs
1/4 cup chopped fresh parsley
1/4 cup milk
1 teaspoon seasoned salt
1/4 teaspoon pepper
1 tablespoon olive oil
1 (28 ounce) can whole
   tomatoes, cut up and
   undrained
1 bay leaf

1/2 teaspoon salt
1/2 teaspoon sugar
1/2 teaspoon fennel seed,
   crushed
1 teaspoon Italian seasoning
1/4 teaspoon thyme leaves
1/2 teaspoon oregano
1/8 teaspoon crushed red pepper
1 (6 ounce) can tomato paste
1 pound package favorite pasta,
   uncooked
Grated Parmesan cheese

In medium bowl, combine first 7 ingredients; mix well. Shape 12 meatballs. In Dutch oven, brown meatballs in oil. Add remaining ingredients, except pasta and Parmesan cheese. Bring to boil. Reduce heat; simmer, covered, 30 minutes, stirring occasionally.

Prepare your favorite pasta according to package directions; drain. Serve with meatballs and sauce. Top with Parmesan cheese.

Venison Meat
With Spaghetti Sauce

1 pound venison (cubed)
½ pound sausage, bulk
2 tablespoons olive oil
½ small onion, diced
½ green pepper, diced
2 stalks celery, diced
3 or 4 bay leaves, broken up fine
2 to 3 cloves garlic, diced
1 teaspoon red pepper (optional)
2 tablespoons chili powder

1 (28 ounce) can tomatoes
1 (8 ounce) can tomato sauce
1 (6 ounce) can tomato paste
½ teaspoon oregano
½ teaspoon rosemary
¼ teaspoon fennel seeds
1 (4 ounce) can mushrooms
Grated Romano or Parmesan
    cheese

Cook venison and sausage together until brown. Then add onion, green pepper, celery, bay leaves, garlic, red pepper, and chili powder. Cook until vegetables are tender. Add tomatoes, tomato sauce and tomato paste. Allow to simmer 2 or 3 hours. When sauce boils down add water. About 30 minutes before serving add the oregano, rosemary, fennel seeds and mushrooms.

Cook one pound spaghetti in salted boiling water about 20 minutes. Place pasta in serving bowl and top with venison pasta sauce. Sprinkle with grated Romano or Parmesan cheese. Now that is yummy Italian!

Ziti With Venison Sauce

1 pound ground venisonburger
1 cup onion, chopped
1 (16 ounce) can stewed
   tomatoes
1 teaspoon garlic powder
2 (8 ounce) cans tomato sauce
1 cup black olives, coarsely
   chopped

¼ cup Parmesan cheese wedge,
   grated
1 teaspoon seasoned salt
½ teaspoon oregano leaves
¼ teaspoon crushed red pepper
1 (1 pound) package ziti pasta
2 tablespoons softened butter
1 cup Mozzarella cheese, grated

In large skillet cook ground venison and onion. Add tomatoes, garlic powder, tomato sauce, olives, Parmesan cheese, seasoned salt, oregano, and crushed pepper. Simmer 15 minutes. Prepare pasta according to package directions. Drain. Toss with softened butter. Arrange in a 3-quart shallow baking dish; pour on meat sauce; top with Mozzarella. Place under broiler 2 to 3 minutes until cheese melts.

Venison Rigatoni Bake

1 pound venisonburger or
   sausage
1 medium onion, chopped
1 (16 ounce) can tomatoes, cut
   up, undrained
1 (8 ounce) can tomato sauce
½ cup sliced pitted ripe olives
½ cup grated Parmesan cheese
1 teaspoon salt

½ teaspoon oregano leaves
¼ teaspoon crushed red pepper
½ teaspoon black pepper
1 cup chili or picante sauce
1 (1 pound) package Rigatoni,
   uncooked
2 tablespoons butter
1 cup (4 ounces) shredded
   mozzarella cheese

In large skillet, cook ground venison and onion until venison is browned; drain. Stir in tomatoes, tomato sauce, olives, Parmesan cheese, salt, oregano, crushed red pepper, black pepper and chili or picante sauce. Bring to boil. Reduce heat; simmer 30 minutes. Prepare Rigatoni according to package directions; drain. Add butter; toss to coat. Spread Rigatoni in a 3 quart casserole; top with hot meat sauce. Top evenly with mozzarella cheese. Broil just until cheese melts, 2 to 3 minutes. Garlic bread, anyone?

Our family really likes the savory richness venison adds to any homemade pasta dish. Try this "Spicy Venison Pasta Sauce" soon and see if it does not become one of your favorite pasta sauces, too.

Spicy Venison Pasta Sauce

1 pound venisonburger or
    venison sausage
2 tablespoons olive oil
2 green onions, chopped
1 small onion, chopped
2 to 3 garlic cloves, diced
½ teaspoon oregano

½ teaspoon salt
½ teaspoon red pepper
½ teaspoon parsley
½ teaspoon Italian seasoning
½ teaspoon black pepper
1 (26 to 32 ounce) jar pasta
    sauce
1 pound any pasta

In a Dutch oven, brown venison for about 15 minutes in two tablespoons of olive oil along with onions and garlic. Add next 6 spices and brown 10 minutes. Add 1 jar of your favorite store bought pasta sauce. Add one half jar water to venison pasta sauce and simmer an hour or so. Delicious over one pound favorite pasta. Enjoy.

Venison Sausage Italian Bean Soup

2 teaspoons olive oil
1 pound bulk venison sausage
2 cloves garlic, diced
1 cup chopped onion
1 (28 ounce) can tomatoes,
    crushed
3½ cups water
2 cubes beef bouillon
1 cup (4 ounces) small elbow
    macaroni, uncooked
1 (16 ounce) can kidney beans,
    drained
2 tablespoons Parmesan cheese

In soup kettle or 4 quart saucepan heat oil over medium heat. Add sausage, garlic, and onion; saute 5 minutes, stirring occasionally. Add tomatoes (with juices), water and bouillon; bring to a boil. Add pasta, beans and cheese. Reduce heat to low, cover and simmer until pasta is tender, about 15 minutes. Pass the hot biscuits, please!

Homestyle Venison Pasta Sauce

1 tablespoon olive oil
1 pound venison steak, sliced
    thin
1 medium onion, chopped
2 large cloves garlic, minced
1 cup water
³/₄ teaspoon salt
½ teaspoon dried oregano
1 (28 ounce) can crushed
    tomatoes
1 teaspoon sugar
½ teaspoon dried basil
¼ teaspoon pepper
1 cup salsa or chili sauce

In a 3-quart Dutch oven heat olive oil over medium-high heat. Add venison, onion, and garlic. Brown 10 to 15 minutes. Add remaining ingredients; bring to boil. Reduce heat. Cover and simmer, stirring occasionally, 60 minutes. Serve over favorite pasta.

Venison Pasta
With Tomato And Cream Sauce

1 pound or less of your favorite
   pasta
1 pound venisonburger or
   sausage, thinly sliced
   venison steak can be used
   also
2 to 3 tablespoons olive oil

1 medium onion, diced
2 cloves garlic, diced
2 tomatoes, stemmed and diced
1 cup light cream
2 tablespoon Italian seasoning
1 teaspoon salt
½ teaspoon black pepper

In your Dutch oven with lightly salted boiling water cook pasta until tender.

In a large frying pan brown venison 10 to 15 minutes and set aside. Add 2 to 3 tablespoons olive oil to pan, while the pasta cooks, and saute onion and garlic until soft. Add fresh tomatoes to pan and cook 2 to 3 minutes. Stir in cream and simmer 2 minutes before adding Italian seasoning and salt and pepper to taste. Add venison back and cook 10 minutes.

Serve venison pasta sauce over as much as one pound of your favorite pasta in a large serving bowl. Pass the Parmesan cheese, please!

Venison Parmesan

1 (1 pound) package Ziti or
   pasta
¼ cup olive oil
¼ cup chopped green bell
   pepper
2 cloves garlic, minced
1 pound venison sausage
6 green onions, chopped

2 tablespoons all-purpose flour
1 (15 ounce) can whole
   tomatoes, chopped,
   undrained
½ teaspoon salt
½ teaspoon pepper
½ cup grated Parmesan cheese

Cook Ziti or pasta as package directs; drain. In a large skillet, heat olive oil. Add green pepper, garlic, venison, and onion. Saute until venison is browned. Stir in flour. Add tomatoes, salt, and pepper; simmer 30 minutes. Spoon meat sauce over pasta. Sprinkle with Parmesan cheese.

Venison Mozzarella

1 tablespoon olive oil
1 pound venison steak, thinly
   sliced
1 (14½ ounce) can tomato sauce
   (Italian style)

4 thick slices (3 ounces)
   mozzarella cheese
Hot cooked pasta or rice

Heat olive oil in large skillet over medium-high heat. Add venison; brown 10 to 11 minutes on each side or until golden brown; drain. Pour tomatoes and juice over venison. Bring to a boil. Reduce heat to medium-low; cover. Cook for 20 to 25 minutes or until venison is tender. Place cheese over venison and tomatoes; cover. Cook for 1 to 2 minutes or until cheese is melted. Pour over pasta or rice. Ah!

Tasty Venison And Pasta Sauce

1 pound venisonburger or bulk
    sausage
2 green peppers, diced
2 medium onions, diced
2 (15 ounce) cans tomato sauce
1 (6 ounce) can tomato paste
1/2 cup water
1 (4 ounce) can sliced
    mushrooms, drained

1 tablespoon Worcestershire
    sauce
1 teaspoon basil leaves
1 teaspoon salt
1/2 teaspoon pepper
1/2 teaspoon garlic powder
1 pound package favorite pasta

In a large skillet fry venisonburger or sausage until almost brown. Add green pepper and onion, cook until tender. Stir in tomato sauce, tomato paste, water, mushrooms, Worcestershire, basil, salt, pepper and garlic powder. Simmer uncovered 20 minutes. Prepare pasta according to package directions. Drain. Arrange pasta on large platter and pour on sauce.

Italian Cannellini Beans With Venison Sausage And Tomato Sauce

4 cups dried cannellini beans
    or 1 (32 ounce) can beans
Salt for large pot of water
1/2 cup olive oil
1/4 cup onion, chopped
2 cloves garlic, diced
1 teaspoon sage

1 (14 ounce) can chopped
    Italian tomatoes, undrained
1 teaspoon salt
1 teaspoon Italian seasoning
1 teaspoon black pepper
1 pound venison sausage
1/2 cup red wine

Soak beans overnight if using dried beans. Cook in large pot of salted water 2 hours. Heat oil in Dutch oven; add onion and garlic and saute for flavor. Add drained beans or canned beans, sage and tomatoes. Season with salt, Italian seasoning, and pepper. Bring to a boil, then simmer 20 minutes, or until sauce is thick, adding water if needed. Saute sausage in dry skillet until partly cooked, about 10 minutes. Cook sausage in pan with red wine. Cook until liquid is reduced by half, about 5 minutes, and serve over beans. Stir well and enjoy!

Cooking Venison Crockery Style

It is not necessary to saute vegetables first for recipes. Just cut them and drop them in the crock and place seasoned meat on top of them. Add more seasoning and vegetables if called for.

The low moist heat of the crockery or slow cooker is ideal for tenderizing tougher cuts of venison like ribs, hocks and front shoulder roasts. Unlike in conventional cooking liquids do not cook away. So lean venison cooks up moist and tender. If you have a work day planned when using a crock pot recipe, we suggest you prepare the meat and vegetables the night before and put the meal together the next morning before work.

Despite the venison's flavorful aroma during cooking, resist the temptation to lift the lid during cooking. It allows significant heat to escape so each time it extends the recipe cooking time.

Enjoy our recipes and never be afraid to experiment with your favorite seasonings or adding your favorite sauces or gravies. When you start a recipe with quality venison you cannot go too far wrong.

Easy Venison Stew

3 cups water
1 can mushroom or cream of
   broccoli soup
1 pound venison steak, cubed
   into bite-size pieces and
   browned
1 package beef stew seasoning
   mix

2 cloves garlic, diced
4 to 5 chopped carrots
1 quart stewed tomatoes
2 chopped onions
1 cup butter beans or lima
   beans
4 potatoes, chopped

Mix all ingredients in crock pot and cook on low heat 6 to 7 hours. Add water if needed.

Clyde's Italian Venison Soup

1 to 1¼ pounds venison stew
   meat, cut in small cubes
2 cups fresh tomatoes, chopped
½ cup onion, chopped
2 to 3 cloves garlic, diced
4 to 6 ounces mushrooms, sliced
½ cup red wine
2 (14½ ounce) cans beef broth
1 teaspoon salt

1 teaspoon black pepper
1 cup green peppers, sliced
1 cup fresh carrots, chopped
1 cup lima beans
1 tablespoon Italian seasoning
½ cup Parmesan cheese
½ cup favorite rice
1 cup water

Add cubed venison to your crock pot/slow cooker. Prepare tomatoes, onion, garlic, and mushrooms and add to crock pot. Add wine and broth; stir well. Add salt, pepper, green pepper, carrots, lima beans and Italian seasoning. Stir well. Set cooker on low and simmer 6 hours. Then add ½ cup Parmesan cheese, ½ cup rice and 1 cup water. Cover and simmer 2 hours more. Stir well and serve in large bowls. Deliciously nutritious!!

Crocky Venison Roast

3 to 4 pounds venison roast
$\frac{1}{3}$ to $\frac{1}{2}$ cup butter for browning
1 can onion soup

1 can cream of broccoli soup
3 cloves garlic, diced
1 large onion sliced

Brown roast in butter in frying pan on all sides. Remove roast and place in crock pot. Pour one can of onion soup and one can of cream of broccoli soup over roast. Add garlic and onion and cook on low for 8 hours. You'll have a venison roast and gravy that's great!

Maybe it is our personal enjoyment of eating venison barbecue that makes the Crock Pot Venison Roast recipe one of our delicious annual favorites. Try it and see if you do not agree. Venison barbecue in January seems like a tasty dish — think Spring!

Crock Pot Venison Roast

2 to 3 pounds venison round
    steak or roast
1 teaspoon chili powder
$\frac{1}{2}$ teaspoon garlic powder
$\frac{1}{2}$ teaspoon pepper
Barbecue Sauce:
1 stalk celery, chopped
$\frac{1}{2}$ cup catsup

$\frac{1}{2}$ cup chili sauce
2 teaspoons garlic, diced
$\frac{1}{4}$ cup packed brown sugar
2 tablespoons vinegar
2 tablespoons Worcestershire
    sauce
$1\frac{1}{2}$ teaspoons liquid smoke
1 teaspoon dry mustard

Combine chili powder, garlic powder, and pepper; rub evenly over meat. Cut venison roast to fit into crock pot. Place meat in a $3\frac{1}{2}$ to 4 or 5 quart crock pot. For barbecue sauce, combine celery, catsup, chili sauce, garlic, brown sugar, vinegar, Worcestershire sauce, liquid smoke, and dry mustard. Pour over venison in crock pot. Cover; cook on low heat setting for 8 to 10 hours or on high heat setting for 4 to 5 hours. Remove meat from cooker. Cut venison into thin slices and serve with sauce. Serve with salad and baked beans and garlic bread. Hungry?

Pot-Roasted Venison In Red Wine

3 to 4 pounds venison, choice
   roast
1 (14½ ounce) can beef broth
3 cloves garlic, chopped
½ teaspoon parsley
½ teaspoon oregano
½ teaspoon black pepper

½ cup butter
2 cups dry red wine
2 medium-size onions, sliced
2 bay leaves
1 tablespoon Italian seasoning
½ teaspoon celery salt
1 teaspoon salt

Mix all ingredients together, except venison. Then pour marinade over meat in Dutch oven and let stand 1 to 2 days in refrigerator. Turn venison 2 times a day. Take meat out of marinade, drain well. Sear in hot butter until brown on all sides. Put in slow cooker, pour marinade over venison. Simmer on low in slow cooker for 8 to 10 hours. For gravy, mix 3 tablespoons of crock pot liquid with 3 tablespoons flour; add to hot liquid and cook 30 minutes. Before serving add salt, if needed.

Slow Cooker Venison Pasta Sauce

1½ pounds venison steak,
   cubed
1½ pounds ground
   venisonburger or sausage
3 tablespoons olive oil
2 tablespoons chili powder
2 large or 3 medium onions,
   sliced thin
1 teaspoon black pepper
2 teaspoons salt
2 teaspoons spicy brown
   mustard

1 (28 to 32 ounce) jar of your
   favorite store bought pasta
   sauce
3 bay leaves
4 garlic cloves, diced
3 stalks celery, chopped
1 tablespoon Italian seasoning
1 teaspoon red pepper flakes
2 (6 ounce) cans tomato paste,
   your choice
4 ounces fresh mushrooms
1 green pepper, chopped
2½ cups water

Brown cubed steak and ground meat in olive oil in a Dutch oven for 20 to 25 minutes. Add venison and the remainder of the ingredients to slow cooker. Cover cooker and cook on high for 4 to 6 hours, adding more water if desired. Serve over favorite pasta and freeze extra sauce. That's Italian!

This recipe, "Crock Pot Duck and Venison," was prepared several years ago for the first time when we were going to entertain friends over an Easter weekend. Unfortunately our freezer was low on game and we had to use one duck and one venison roast in the same recipe if we were going to treat our guests to a gourmet game dinner. It worked. Delicious — taste and see!

Crock Pot And Venison

1 large wild mallard duck*
1½ pounds venison roast
1 cup beef broth
2 celery stalks, chopped
2 cloves garlic, chopped
1 teaspoon black pepper
1 teaspoon parsley
1 cup fresh mushrooms, chopped
2 carrots, chopped
1 onion, sliced
1 teaspoon salt
1 teaspoon Italian seasoning
1 cup red wine

With game shears or knife cut duck into breasts, legs, and wings. Set aside and cut venison into chunks; then add venison and duck to crock pot or Dutch oven. Set crock pot/Dutch oven to high or simmering temperature and add remaining ingredients except red wine.

Cook on high in crock pot or simmer in Dutch oven for 3 hours. Then 1 cup red wine is added and turn cock pot to low and/ or Dutch oven to slow simmer and cook for 2 to 3 hours until tender. Serve with your favorite rice, potatoes, vegetables and hot bread or biscuits. Enjoy! Delicious!

*Use 3 to 4 pounds venison if you do not have a duck.

Steubenville Venison Stew

2 pounds deer meat, cubed
½ cup water
1 cup grape juice or jelly
1 bay leaf
2 cloves garlic, minced
1 teaspoon salt
1 teaspoon pepper
2 tablespoons olive oil

1 (14½ ounce) can beef broth
2 stalks celery, diced
1 teaspoon Italian seasoning
1 teaspoon chopped parsley
½ teaspoon thyme
2 carrots, sliced
1 small onion, sliced

Combine water , grape jelly or grape juice, bay leaf, garlic, salt and pepper in a large dish; stir. Add cubed meat and refrigerate for several hours, turning meat frequently. Reserving grape liquid, drain meat and brown on all sides in olive oil before placing it in slow cooker. Stir in grape liquid, broth; combine celery, Italian seasoning, parsley and thyme in your slow cooker. Add venison and simmer on low setting for 8 hours, or until tender. During last ½ hour of cooking; add carrots and onions. Thicken gravy, if desired, with 3 tablespoons flour mixed with 1 cup water. Add to venison.

The crock pot has done such a nice job at creating savory slow cooked venison dishes for us over the years. While all the slow cooker recipes in this section are delicious, "Lansdale Slow Cooker Venison" is especially tasty. Give it a try soon and you will see!

Lansdale Slow Cooker Venison

2½ to 3 pounds venison roast, cubed
2 carrots, chopped
1 onion, sliced
1 teaspoon salt
1 teaspoon Italian seasoning
2 cups beef broth or beef bouillon

2 celery stalks, chopped
2 cloves garlic, chopped
1 teaspoon black pepper
1 teaspoon parsley
1 cup fresh mushrooms, chopped
1 cup red wine with 2 tablespoons flour

Cut venison into chunks; then add venison to crock pot and add remaining ingredients except red wine. Cook on high in crock pot for 3 hours. Then to 1 cup red wine add 2 tablespoons flour and mix; add to crock pot for gravy. Turn crock pot to low; cook for 2 to 3 hours or until tender. Serve with your favorite rice, potatoes, vegetable and hot bread or biscuits. Enjoy! Delicious!

Crock Pot Venison Burgundy

2 pounds venison, cut in strips
4 slices bacon
2 cloves garlic, diced
12 ounces mushrooms, sliced
½ bunch green onions, sliced
3 tablespoons butter
⅓ cup butter
1 cup flour

1½ cans beef broth
1½ cups burgundy wine
1 bay leaf
1 tablespoon chopped parsley
Salt, thyme and pepper to taste
1 carrot, sliced
1 stalk celery, sliced

Chop bacon and brown in large frying pan; then set bacon aside. Brown venison in bacon drippings, stirring often. Then put venison and bacon in crock pot. Saute garlic cloves, mushrooms, and onions in 3 tablespoons of butter in skillet and add to crock pot. Melt ⅓ cup butter in frying pan and add flour. Cook and stir until the flour is a light brown. Then add it, the beef broth and burgundy wine, bay leaf, chopped parsley, and sprinkle generously with salt, thyme, and pepper all to the crock pot. Add carrots and celery to crock pot; cover and simmer on high 6½ hours, or until the venison is tender. Additional wine or water may be added, when necessary, to keep meat moist. AH!

Crock Pot Deer

2 pounds deer, cut into bite-
　　sized pieces
1 pound venison or pork
　　sausage
1 cup flour
1 teaspoon salt
1 teaspoon pepper
1 cup vegetable oil

2 cups beef broth
3 potatoes, diced
1 package onion soup mix
1½ cups water
1 can cream of broccoli soup
1 onion, diced
1 (4 ounce) can mushrooms

Roll deer pieces in flour seasoned with salt and pepper. Heat vegetable oil in a frying pan and brown deer pieces and venison or pork sausage. Combine deer pieces and crumbled sausage with other ingredients into a crock pot. Cook on low for 6 to 8 hours.

Venison Crocked Round Steaks With Herby Mushrooms

2 pounds venison round steak, cut 1 inch thick
1 tablespoon olive oil
1 medium onion, sliced
2 cups sliced fresh mushrooms
2 cloves garlic, diced
1 (10³⁄₄ ounce) can condensed cream of celery or nacho cheese soup
¹⁄₄ cup dry white wine

¹⁄₂ teaspoon dried oregano, crushed
¹⁄₂ teaspoon dried thyme, crushed
¹⁄₂ teaspoon pepper
¹⁄₂ teaspoon parsley
3 cups hot cooked noodles or rice

Cut venison into serving size portions. In a large skillet brown venison on both sides in hot oil. In a 3¹⁄₂ or 4 quart slow cooker place onion slices and mushrooms. Place venison on top of vegetables, and top steak with diced garlic. In a small bowl combine soup, wine, oregano, thyme, pepper and parsley; pour over venison. Cover; cook on low heat setting for 8 to 10 hours or on high heat setting for 4 to 5 hours. Serve over hot cook noodles or rice. And pass the garlic bread, please!

Crock Pot Venison

2 to 3 pounds venison rump roast, sliced
¹⁄₂ cup flour
1¹⁄₂ teaspoons salt
¹⁄₂ teaspoon pepper
1 cup olive oil
1 can cream of mushroom soup
1 can cream of celery soup

2 stalks celery, chopped
1 onion, chopped
1 cup fresh mushrooms, sliced
4 green bell peppers, sliced
1¹⁄₂ cups water
¹⁄₂ cup red wine
1 tablespoon parsley
¹⁄₂ teaspoon black pepper

Dredge steaks in seasoned flour, salt and pepper. In small amount of olive oil, brown on both sides and place in crock pot. Add remaining ingredients and cook for 7 to 8 hours on high heat. Serve over rice, noodles or baked potato.

Ever wonder what would be an easy way to cook venison shanks for a great meal? Lamonte, a southern friend of mine shared this recipe I call "Rebel Venison Soup." It is a tasty recipe for tough venison like the shanks so they do not go to waste. Enjoy!

Rebel Venison Soup

4 venison shanks or 2 hind quarter hocks, cut into small chunks, about 1½ pounds
2 quarts tomato juice
3 onions, sliced
¼ cup soy sauce
3 garlic cloves, diced
2 bay leaves
2 tablespoons paprika
2 tablespoons chili powder
1 teaspoon parsley
1 teaspoon black pepper
½ teaspoon cayenne pepper
½ cup bottled barbecue sauce
1 (10 ounce) package frozen okra

Add 1 quart tomato juice to slow cooker and add venison chunks. Add chopped onions, soy sauce, and garlic. Now add spices, favorite barbecue sauce, and frozen okra. Set slow cooker to low and cook for 6 to 8 hours. Great dish with your choice of bread and salad or serve soup over rice or noodles.

Ah, "Venison Jambalaya!" This recipe was created because of our appreciation for Cajun food. Cajun food varies from hot and very spicy to mildly seasoned soups and stews. Gumbo, Jambalaya, Creole dishes use wild game, fish, shrimp, sausage and rice to create delicious dishes. Try this special dish. Enjoy!

Venison Jambalaya

1 pound chopped venison steak, cut into ½ inch cubes
1½ cups brown rice
1 (28 ounce) can diced, peeled tomatoes, with their liquid
¾ cup Burgundy wine
3 celery ribs, chopped
2 medium onions, chopped
1 green bell pepper, chopped
1 (10 ounce) package frozen okra or broccoli

2 tablespoons chopped fresh parsley
1 teaspoon Italian seasoning
½ teaspoon garlic, diced
¼ to ½ teaspoon cayenne
½ teaspoon seasoned salt
½ teaspoon freshly ground black pepper
1 teaspoon dried basil
½ to 1 pound peeled and deveined cooked shrimp

In 3½ or 4 quart slow cooker, mix the venison, rice, tomatoes, wine, celery, onions, bell pepper, okra, parsley, Italian seasoning, garlic, cayenne, seasoned salt and black pepper. Cover and cook on low heat setting 4 to 5 hours, or until rice is tender but not sticky and mushy. Stir in basil and shrimp. Cook, covered, 20 to 30 minutes longer until heated through.

Venison Pot Roast With Noodles

1 (2 to 2½ pound) venison
    quarter roast
1 tablespoon olive oil
3 medium carrots, coarsely
    chopped
2 stalks celery, sliced
1 medium onion, sliced
2 cloves garlic, minced
1 tablespoon Italian seasoning

1 (14½ ounce) can Italian-style
    stewed tomatoes
1 (6 ounce) can Italian-style
    tomato paste
1 tablespoon brown sugar
1 teaspoon salt
½ teaspoon pepper
1 bay leaf
4 cups hot cooked noodles or
    rice

If necessary, cut roast to fit into crockery cooker. In a large skillet brown roast on all sides in olive oil. Meanwhile, in a 3½ or 4 quart crockery cooker place carrots, celery, onion, and garlic. Place meat atop vegetables. In a bowl combine Italian seasoning, undrained tomatoes, tomato paste, brown sugar, salt, pepper and bay leaf; pour over the meat. Cover and cook on low heat setting for 10 to 12 hours or on high heat setting for 4 to 5 hours. Discard bay leaf. Serve with hot cooked noodles or rice.

Slow-Cooker Venison And Vegetable Rice

2 to 2½ pound boneless venison
    shoulder meat
1 tablespoon olive oil
2½ cups tomato juice
1 cup regular brown rice
1 teaspoon chili powder
½ teaspoon red pepper flakes
1 teaspoon salt

½ teaspoon black pepper
2 celery stalks, chopped
2 medium carrots, cut into ½
    inch pieces
2 cloves garlic, diced
1 medium green sweet pepper
    cut into ½ inch strips

Trim fat from venison shoulder. In a large skillet brown meat on all sides in hot oil. Meanwhile, in a 3½ or 4 quart crock pot combine tomato juice, uncooked rice, chili powder, red pepper flakes, salt and pepper. Add celery and carrots. Place meat atop carrots and celery. Add garlic to top. Cover; cook on low heat setting for 7 to 8 hours or on high heat setting for 3½ to 4 hours. Add the green sweet pepper to the crock pot. Cover and let stand 10 to 15 minutes.

If your family likes a hearty, flavorful soup in the cold winter months following the deer season, then you must prepare this "Italian Minestrone with Venison" recipe. You will want to cook it again and again. Do not hesitate to change the fresh vegetables around to make it different or improved to your liking. It is the rich venison that makes it so flavorful again and again.

Italian Minestrone With Venison

1½ pounds venison, cubed
⅓ cup olive oil
1 teaspoon Italian seasoning
1 cup chopped green onions
3 cloves garlic, minced
6 cups beef broth
½ cup dry red wine
1 (16 ounce) can tomatoes, undrained

2 cups thinly sliced carrots
1 cup thinly sliced celery
1 cup salsa or chili sauce
2 cups sliced zucchini
4 ounces mushrooms, sliced
1 medium green pepper, diced
¼ cup chopped fresh parsley
Grated Parmesan cheese

In a large frying pan brown cubed venison in ⅓ cup olive oil 10 to 15 minutes with Italian seasoning, onions and garlic. Drain any excess oil or fat. Add to 3 to 5 quart crock pot. Add beef broth, wine, tomatoes, carrots, celery, salsa or chili sauce. Stir in zucchini, mushrooms, green pepper and parsley. Cook on high for 5 to 6 hours and low for 6 to 8 hours. Top soup with cheese just before serving. Pass the garlic bread, and please enjoy!

A DEER HUNTER'S WIFE KNOWS!
While a buck trophy mount is impressive to some people it does not feed ANY PEOPLE...not family, friends or the needy in your community. Steve says it is best to harvest the legal deer that God presents us with, cleanly, and accurately. There is always next year to take a bigger antlered buck.

Sloppy Joes
Of Venison

1½ pounds ground
　venisonburger
1 cup chopped onion
2 cloves garlic, minced
1 cup chili sauce
½ cup chopped green sweet
　pepper
¾ cup chopped celery
¼ cup water

1 to 2 tablespoons brown sugar
2 tablespoons prepared
　mustard
2 tablespoons wine or vinegar
2 tablespoons Worcestershire
　sauce
1½ teaspoons chili powder
½ teaspoon parsley flakes
8 hamburger buns, split

In a Dutch oven or a large skillet cook ground venison, onion, and garlic until meat is brown and onion is tender. Meanwhile, in a 3½ or 4 quart crockery cooker combine chili sauce, green pepper, celery, water, brown sugar, mustard, vinegar or wine, Worcestershire sauce, chili powder, and parsley. Stir in meat mixture. Cover and cook on low heat setting for 6 to 8 hours or on high heat setting for 3 to 4 hours. Spoon into buns. Great snack with chips and Buffalo wings. Enjoy!

'Slow Cooker'
Italian-Style Venison Meat Loaf

1 (8 ounce) can tomato sauce
1 beaten egg
½ cup chopped onion
½ cup chopped green sweet
    pepper
⅓ cup fine dry seasoned bread
    crumbs

1 clove garlic, diced
¼ teaspoon pepper
½ teaspoon fennel seed,
    crushed (optional)
1½ pounds ground
    venisonburger
½ cup shredded mozzarella
    cheese (2 ounces or so)

Reserve ⅓ cup tomato sauce; cover and chill. In a medium mixing bowl combine remaining tomato sauce and egg. Stir in onion, green sweet pepper, bread crumbs, garlic, pepper, and fennel seed. Add ground venisonburger and mix well.

Crisscross three 18x2-inch foil strips (atop a sheet of waxed paper to keep counter clean). In center of the foil strips shape a 6-inch round meat loaf. Bringing up foil strips, lift and transfer meat and foil to a 3½, 4, or 5 quart crockery cooker. Press meat away from sides of the cooker to avoid burning.

Cover; cook on low heat setting for 7 to 9 hours or on high heat setting for 3½ to 4½ hours (or to 170 degree internal temperature).

Spread meat with the reserved ⅓ cup tomato sauce. Sprinkle top with mozzarella cheese. Cover cooker and let stand 10 to 15 minutes. Then using foil strips, carefully lift meat loaf and transfer to a serving plate; discard the foil strips. Slice loaf. Add baked sweet potatoes and butter. Enjoy!

A DEER HUNTER'S WIFE KNOWS!
If you are ever unfortunate enough to be out of your supply of venison, you can prepare one of our easy recipes by substituting a similar amount of meat; understanding there are fat content differences to drain when necessary. Although the meal will not taste as good as if it were made with venison, it will still be tasty for your family and friends.

This "Royal Venison Roast" recipe is so delicious that it has been used off and on yearly for the past eight years. We usually use the football shaped sirloin tip roast that comes from the hind quarter, but the top round or rump roast will do fine. For a special meal occasion you will want to prepare this dish.

Royal Venison Roast

3 to 4 pounds boneless venison rump roast
1/2 cup all-purpose flour
1 to 2 tablespoons olive oil
1 teaspoon salt
1 teaspoon black pepper
1 bunch green onions, chopped
1 cup Rosé wine
1/2 cup water
1/2 cup picante sauce

2 cloves garlic, minced
1/2 teaspoon parsley
1 teaspoon Italian seasoning
1/4 teaspoon dried basil
1/4 teaspoon dry mustard
1 small bay leaf
1 cup mushrooms, sliced
1/2 cup cold water
1/4 cup all purpose flour
Noodles or rice

Dredge venison in 1/2 cup flour; brown on all sides in oil. Place venison in a 3 1/2 to 4 quart crock pot. Season with salt and black pepper. Add onion. Combine wine, 1/2 cup water, picante sauce, and next 6 ingredients. Pour over meat. Cover and simmer on high heat 6 to 7 hours. Add mushrooms. Blend 1/2 cup cold water and 1/4 cup flour until smooth; add to crock pot and cook 1 to 2 more hours on high heat depending on age of the venison. Discard bay leaf. Serve roast and gravy on bed of cooked rice or noodles. Tender and so tasty. Enjoy!

Venison And Vegetable Stew

1 pound boneless venison steak
   cut in ¾ inch cubes
1 tablespoon olive oil
2½ cups beef broth
2 stalks celery, chopped
1 large onion, cut into wedges
2 medium carrots, thinly sliced
½ green pepper, chopped,
   (½ cup)
2 medium zucchini, halved
   lengthwise, sliced

1 bay leaf
½ teaspoon chili powder
2 cloves garlic, diced
1 teaspoon dried Italian
   seasoning
½ teaspoon pepper
1 (6 ounce) can tomato paste
½ cup water
2 tablespoons flour

In a large frying pan brown cubed venison in a tablespoon of olive oil. To your crock pot add beef broth, venison, vegetables, spices and tomato paste. Cook on a low setting for 6 to 8 hours or on a high setting for 4 to 5 hours. Thicken your stew with half cup water and 2 tablespoons of flour if desired; cook another 30 minutes before serving. Mix well and enjoy a nutritious venison and vegetable meal.

Cooking Venison Traditional Style

Any cut of venison that has been quality cared for from careful field dressing, controlled aging to careful boning, fat trimmed before freezing, and double freezer wrapped is heartily delicious and can be substituted in most beef recipes. Just be sure that since venison is very lean, to keep venison moist during cooking and do not overcook it because it can dry out and get tough. When you prepare your quality cared for venison from recipes in our book or elsewhere it is always delicious. But if venison care from field to freezer leaves a lot to be desired - examples: leave the hide on too long or the deer is exposed to days of warm temperatures, thus improper aging, field dressing mistakes are made, or butcher shortcuts are taken; then even good venison recipes can not help venison that has already gone bad. It is not the fault of the deer, the venison or the recipe. Try these tested venison recipes on your family and friends to enjoy year in and year out.

Mexican Hot Pot

1 pound ground venison or venisonburger
2 teaspoons butter
½ teaspoon cayenne pepper
1 teaspoon paprika or chili powder
1 teaspoon freshly ground black pepper
½ teaspoon ground coriander
3 garlic cloves, minced
½ teaspoon ground cumin
1 medium onion, chopped
1 jalapeno pepper, seeded and minced
1 (14 ounce) can beef broth
1 (16 ounce) package frozen whole-kernel corn
3 medium tomatoes, chopped
2 (10 ounce) baking potatoes, peeled and diced
10 ounces frozen green beans
1 (8 ounce) can kidney beans, rinsed and drained

Fry venison in butter in a large skillet over medium heat. Add cayenne pepper, paprika, black pepper, coriander, garlic cloves, cumin, chopped onion, and jalapeno pepper; saute 5 minutes or until onion is tender. Add broth, corn, tomatoes, and potatoes; reduce heat to low, and simmer, uncovered, 15 to 20 minutes, stirring occasionally. Sir in green beans and kidney beans; simmer 5 minutes or until thoroughly heated. A healthy and tasty meal!

Sally's Venison Meat Loaf

½ pound pork
½ cup chopped onion
¼ cup chopped celery
1 cup soft bread crumbs
1 egg, beaten
1 teaspoon black pepper
2 pounds ground venisonburger
2 cloves garlic, diced
¼ cup chopped parsley
1 cup canned stewed tomatoes
1 teaspoon salt
¼ cup Parmesan or Romano grated cheese

Cut pork in small pieces and fry until lightly browned. Mix with remaining ingredients. Place mixture in loaf pan. Bake in a 350 degree oven 1½ hours. Check venison for doneness. Sprinkle cheese over loaf and bake for another 30 minutes. Just add mashed baked potatoes and your favorite vegetable. Enjoy!

This is an excellent dish for hunting camp. "Hunter's Style Stew" is a dish my dad made occasionally for his customers who were hunters and would give him venison to cook. Add hot buttered bread and a sweet potato on the side and you will have a very delicious meal.

Hunter's Style Stew

$1\frac{1}{2}$ pounds venison stew meat, cubed
$\frac{1}{2}$ teaspoon salt
$\frac{1}{2}$ teaspoon pepper
$\frac{1}{4}$ cup butter
2 cloves garlic, diced
1 onion, chopped
2 cups water
2 beef bouillon cubes
$\frac{3}{4}$ cup red wine

3 to 4 stalks celery, chopped
4 to 5 carrots in 2 inch chunks
$\frac{1}{2}$ teaspoon chili powder
1 bay leaf
$\frac{1}{2}$ teaspoon parsley
$\frac{1}{2}$ cup salsa or chili sauce
2 tablespoons olive oil
2 tablespoons Worcestershire sauce
$1\frac{1}{2}$ teaspoons paprika

Roll cubed venison in flour seasoned with salt and pepper and brown in butter in Dutch oven with garlic and onion. When brown add 2 cups water, bouillon cubes, and wine and bring to a boil. Simmer 1 to $1\frac{1}{2}$ hours. Then add remaining ingredients. Cover and simmer another 45 to 60 minutes so vegetables are tender. Thicken stew to taste with cornstarch mixed with water. Pass the hot bread please. Enjoy!

Easy Venison Steak

1 large venison steak
$\frac{3}{4}$ cup onions, chopped fine
1 clove garlic, diced
2 tablespoons butter
$\frac{1}{2}$ cup water

1 cup mushrooms, chopped
2 tablespoons soy sauce
2 tablespoons flour
$\frac{1}{2}$ cup sour cream

Saute onions and garlic in butter. Add steak and sear on both sides in butter and browned onion and garlic. Add $\frac{1}{2}$ cup water. Cover and let simmer for half an hour. When almost tender, add mushrooms, soy sauce and flour stirred into cream. Cover and let simmer for 20 minutes. Tasty!

Swiss Style Venison Steak

2 to 3 pounds venison round
    steak, cut into ½ or ¾ inch
    slices
½ teaspoon meat tenderizer
½ cup flour
½ to ¾ cup butter
1 onion, sliced
2 garlic cloves, diced

1 to 2 cups water (depends on
    amount of venison)
1½ to 2 teaspoons salt
½ teaspoon pepper
1 bay leaf
¼ teaspoon sweet basil
2 teaspoons Worcestershire
    sauce

Poke the venison with a fork before sprinkling it with the tenderizer. Let stand for about 15 minutes to let the tenderizer work. Then dust the venison with flour and rub it in. Brown venison in butter with onion and garlic. When brown on each side, place in a 3½ quart casserole. Add water and salt and pepper. Bake in 325 degree oven 2 hours. Then add remaining ingredients and more water if necessary. Bake for 1 more hour, if needed, removing the cover the last 15 or 20 minutes to brown. Add more water if juice has evaporated. Remove meat to platter and make gravy.

Virginia Venison Chili

2 pounds ground venisonburger
¼ cup butter
2 (16 ounce) cans kidney beans
2 (8 ounce) cans tomato sauce
3 tablespoons chili powder
½ teaspoon cayenne pepper or
    to taste
1½ cups water

2 cloves garlic, diced
½ teaspoon crushed oregano
1 teaspoon Italian seasoning
1 teaspoon salt
1 teaspoon black pepper
1 cup onion, chopped
1 cup chili or salsa sauce

In a Dutch oven saute venison in butter until brown. Add all ingredients to venison and simmer for 1½ hours, stirring occasionally. Add water if sauce is too thick. Serve piping hot with butter bread or rolls. Hot sauce and cayenne pepper available on request. As always, enjoy!

Steubenville Venison Steak

Cut 1 pound venison steak about ½ inch thick and divide into portions 2 inches square. Season with salt and pepper, place in covered frying pan with 2 tablespoons butter. Brown each side as quickly as possible; then add a dash of cayenne pepper, 2 tablespoons burgundy wine, and 1 tablespoon currant or grape jelly. Let simmer until inside shows only pink when cut. A great steak!

Lazy Day Chili

1 pound ground venison or cubes
1 cup chopped onions
1½ cups chopped bell peppers
2 small cloves garlic, finely chopped
2 cans kidney beans and liquid
Dash red and black pepper (to taste)

1 tablespoon olive oil
1 teaspoon Italian seasoning
2 (14½ ounce) cans stewed tomatoes
2 (8 ounce) cans tomato sauce
2 teaspoons salt
2 tablespoons chili powder
1 cup chopped green onions

Cook meat in heavy pot in oil. Add onions, bell pepper and garlic. Saute. Add remaining ingredients. Bring to boil and stir occasionally. Reduce heat and simmer for 60 minutes to 1½ hours.

Venison And Gravy

1 pound ground venisonburger
½ pound pork bulk sausage
2 cups raw potatoes, diced
1 onion, chopped
1 garlic clove, diced
1½ teaspoons salt
¼ teaspoon pepper

¼ cup milk
3 cups water
2 to 3 tablespoons flour
2 cups sour cream
1 teaspoon Italian seasoning
¼ cup butter

Brown venison and sausage in large skillet. Combine potatoes, onion, garlic, salt, pepper, and milk. Add ½ cup water. Cover. Simmer for 20 to 30 minutes. In remaining 2½ cups water add 2 to 3 tablespoons of flour and blend. Add to skillet and simmer until it thickens. Reduce heat and stir in cream, Italian seasoning and butter. Serve hot with fresh asparagus, rice or noodles.

Ah, we enjoy "Winter Venison Soup" yearly. It is deliciously filled with mostly fresh vegetables. So, add low fat, rich tasting venison and you will enjoy a nutritious dish indeed. Eat heartily with garlic bread or crackers and freeze leftovers for another meal treat.

Winter Venison Soup

2 to 2½ pounds venison, cubed
3 cloves garlic, diced
½ cup butter
3 potatoes, chopped
2 stalks celery, chopped
1 can whole kernel corn
2 (14½ ounce) cans tomatoes
2 teaspoons salt
1 tablespoon parsley
1 beef bouillon cube

½ cup catsup or chili sauce
1 bay leaf
2 carrots, chopped
1 large onion, chopped
10 ounces frozen peas
2 quarts water
½ teaspoon pepper
½ teaspoon garlic salt
1 (4 ounce) can mushrooms
½ green pepper

Brown venison cubes and garlic in Dutch oven with butter for 15 to 20 minutes. Then add remaining ingredients. Simmer for another 40 to 45 minutes.

Venison Chop Suey

1 pound venison, cut into cubes
¼ cup butter or margarine
1 cup onions, chopped
½ teaspoon black pepper
½ teaspoon salt
1 (4 ounce) can mushrooms

2 tablespoons teriyaki sauce
2 tablespoons molasses
2 tablespoons soy sauce
2 cups celery, chopped
1 can bean sprouts
3 tablespoons cornstarch

Brown venison in butter. Add onions, pepper, salt, mushrooms, teriyaki sauce, molasses, soy sauce and celery. Cook for 15 minutes. Drain bean sprouts and reserve liquid. Mix cornstarch in liquid. Add slowly to venison mixture. Cook until thickened. Add bean sprouts. Heat thoroughly. Serve over rice or chow mien noodles.

Baton Rouge Venison Jambalaya

4 slices bacon
1½ pounds ground venison or
    stew meat, cubed
1 (16 ounce) can tomatoes,
    undrained, and cut up
1 pouch onion soup mix
2 cups water
1 medium bay leaf

½ teaspoon hot pepper sauce or
    cayenne pepper
1 cup regular rice, uncooked
1 (6 to 7 ounce) can minced
    clams, drained
1 green pepper, diced
2 to 3 garlic cloves, diced

In 10-inch skillet over medium heat, cook bacon until crisp. Remove to paper towels to drain. Crumble; set aside. In pan drippings brown venison for 10 to 15 minutes. Combine tomatoes, soup mix, water, bay leaf and hot pepper sauce. Heat to boiling. Stir in rice. Reduce heat to low. Cover; simmer 30 minutes, stirring occasionally. Add clams, green pepper and garlic. Cover; cook 30 minutes; remove bay leaf and top with reserved bacon; stir and serve.

Venison Steak In Wine Sauce

2½ to 3 pounds venison round
    steak
2 tablespoons butter
2 to 3 medium onions, chopped
2 garlic cloves, diced
1 cup sliced mushrooms
1 teaspoon black pepper
1 to 2 tablespoons flour

2 tablespoons prepared
    mustard
2 tablespoons Worcestershire
    sauce
1 teaspoon salt
¾ cup red wine
½ cup water

Brown steak on both sides in butter. Add remaining ingredients. Cover tightly and simmer 2 hours. Add mixture of 1 part wine and 2 parts water if needed, during cooking to keep venison moist.

Gravy: Add flour to pan juices and simmer 3 minutes. Add still more liquid if needed. Good with noodles or rice. Enjoy!

Old Time Venison Loin

Sprinkle 2 pounds venison loin steak with salt and pepper and rub well with flour. Place on rack in pan, roast in 400 degree oven half an hour to sear in juices, and then reduce heat to 300 degrees and cover with bacon strips and cook for 20 to 30 minutes more medium rare. Do not add water to pan. Serve with butter and jelly (your choice) sauce, ¼ cup each melted and mixed before serving. Pour over venison before stirring.

As mentioned elsewhere in our book, many of our favorite venison dishes are prepared in Italian style tomato dishes or in barbecue sauce. Our "Buck in Barbecue Sauce" recipe is a family favorite. Maybe it will be a family favorite for your family or deer camp, too!

Buck In Barbecue Sauce

¾ cup olive oil
2 tablespoons spicy mustard
⅓ cup soy sauce
2 tablespoons Worcestershire
    sauce
2 tablespoons red wine
1 cup catsup
3 teaspoons lemon juice
⅓ cup honey
1 tablespoon Italian seasoning

Combine all above ingredients in a small sauce pan, heat to near boiling, lower heat and simmer about 10 to 15 minutes, stirring occasionally. Now ready to use.

Place 2 pounds venison steaks or roast in pieces in glass baking dish and pour sauce over venison to coat thoroughly. Let it marinate for 2 to 4 hours in refrigerator. Bake venison in 350 degree oven for 30 to 35 minutes or until medium rare to medium doneness. Rich tasting and tender venison, too. Goes great with baked sweet potatoes.

Nice weather option: After venison marinates grill it on your water smoker or barbecue grill until cooked to perfection, basting as needed with remaining barbecue sauce. Enjoy with tossed salad and baked or barbecue beans. A family favorite for sure!

Dad's Venison And Bean Goulash

1½ pounds ground venison
½ pound bulk pork sausage
2 cloves garlic, sliced thin
1¼ cups onion, minced
2 green peppers, chopped
1 bouillon cube
1 teaspoon chili powder

1 teaspoon black pepper
4 to 5 dashes hot sauce
2 cups canned tomatoes
2 (16 ounce) cans kidney beans,
  drained
1 cup brown rice

In a Dutch oven brown ground venison and sausage. Add garlic, onion, green peppers, bouillon, and chili powder. Cook five minutes. Add black pepper, hot sauce, tomatoes with juice, and beans. Add 1 cup rice. Stir to blend well. Simmer 1 hour or until rice is tender.

Deer Roast In The Bag

3 to 4 pound deer roast
Large Reynolds cooking bag
1 package dry onion soup mix
2 tablespoons flour

1 cup water
4 carrots, quartered
1 bell pepper, sliced
1 cup celery, chopped

Preheat oven to 375 degrees. Place roast in the Reynolds cooking bag and place the bag in a shallow roasting pan. Sprinkle dry onion soup and flour over meat. Add water, carrots, bell pepper, and celery. Bake at 375 degrees for 2½ hours. Do not forget to poke 5 to 6 slits into top of bag before roasting.

Sportsman's Venison Steak

2 pounds venison steak
Flour, enough to roll steaks in
½ cup butter
1 large onion, sliced
2 to 4 cups water
¼ cup flour

Salt and black pepper to taste
2 teaspoons garlic powder
Chili powder or red pepper
  flakes to taste
1½ teaspoons parsley flakes

Pound steaks to tenderize, if needed, then roll in flour. In a large skillet, melt butter and fry steaks until medium rare. Remove from the skillet and place in a casserole. Use skillet with remaining butter to brown onion. Pour water over the onions and blend in ¼ cup flour. Stir until thick. Season to taste with salt, pepper, garlic powder, chili powder or red pepper flakes and parsley. Pour over steaks in casserole. Bake in 350 degree oven 20 to 30 minutes.

Mississippi Marinated Venison

3 pounds sliced venison, front
   shoulder
½ cup salad oil
2 tablespoons flour
Marinade:
1 teaspoon parsley
1 bay leaf

1 medium onion, sliced
Butter or olive oil
1 cup dry red wine
2 cloves garlic, crushed
1 teaspoon dried Italian
   seasoning
2 teaspoons black pepper

Combine all ingredients except venison, oil and flour. Marinate the venison in this mixture overnight. Drain and pat dry. Saute the meat in a little butter or oil until brown. Arrange in a baking dish. Strain the marinade and heat to boiling. Thicken with the flour mixed with ¼ cup water. Pour over venison, and bake in a 350 degree oven for 2 to 2½ hours. Serve with your favorite bread, rice and tossed salad.

This recipe, "Mom's Easy Venison Stroganoff," we found to be our daughter's favorite. She will even prepare it for us if we have not had it recently. You will never want hamburger helper again after you have tasted this venison dish.

Mom's Easy Venison Stroganoff

1½ pounds ground
   venisonburger
2 tablespoons minced onion
½ tablespoon parsley flakes
¼ teaspoon garlic powder
1 teaspoon salt
¼ to ½ teaspoon pepper

1 cup fresh mushrooms, sliced
1 can cream of celery or broccoli
   soup
1 cup sour cream
½ cup milk
1 teaspoon Italian seasoning
2 tablespoons soy sauce

Brown venison with onion, parsley and garlic powder. Stir in salt, pepper, mushrooms, and soup. Simmer 15 minutes. Blend in sour cream, milk, Italian seasoning and soy sauce. Heat thoroughly. Serve over noodles or rice. A tasty dish!

Venison Roast
With Herbed Burgundy Gravy

2½ to 3 pound venison roast or stew meat
1 tablespoon olive oil
½ cup chopped onion
½ cup Burgundy wine
½ cup catsup or chili sauce
2 tablespoons Worcestershire sauce
1 teaspoon dried thyme, crushed
1 teaspoon dried oregano, crushed
2 cloves garlic, minced
4 cups hot cooked noodles or rice

If necessary, cut roast to fit into crock pot. In a large skillet brown roast on all sides in hot oil. Transfer the meat to a 3½ or 4 quart crock pot. In a bowl combine onion, Burgundy wine, catsup, Worcestershire, thyme, oregano, and garlic. Pour over venison. Cover and cook on low heat setting for 8 to 10 hours or on high heat setting for 4 to 5 hours. Transfer venison to a serving platter. Pass gravy with meat. Serve with hot cooked noodles or rice.

Broiled Venison Steaks

2 to 2½ pounds venison steaks
⅓ cup lemon juice
1 teaspoon Italian seasoning
1 teaspoon salt
1 cup olive oil
½ cup onions, chopped
1 teaspoon black pepper
2 bay leaves

Put all the above marinade ingredients in a glass bowl or Dutch oven. Mix well and add venison. Marinate 12 to 24 hours turning occasionally. When ready to cook: Broil venison in broiler at 450 degrees 5 minutes, then brush with marinade before broiling other side 5 minutes. Check steak for desired doneness. Best medium rare to medium. Pass the mashed potatoes and fresh corn, please.

Optional: Grill venison steaks outdoors on your grill to taste.

Venison Loin Chops And Dressing

6 venison loin chops
Dressing:
4 cups dry bread crumbs
3 tablespoons chopped onion
1 teaspoon salt
¼ teaspoon pepper

1 teaspoon garlic powder
¼ teaspoon poultry seasoning
⅓ cup melted butter
Sage to taste
Hot water or stock to moisten
1 teaspoon parsley

Combine dressing ingredients and toss gently to mix. Grease baking dish on the bottom. Put in 3 venison chops and then add dressing. Put 3 chops on top and bake in oven one hour at 350 degrees. Serve with favorite vegetables.

You must try this savory venison recipe. Easy to prepare and nutritious, too, for your family or deer camp. Add baked white or sweet potatoes and enjoy!

Dad's Onion-Roasted Venison

4 pound rump or shoulder roast
½ stick butter
½ teaspoon salt
1 teaspoon pepper
1 package dry onion-soup mix
1 cup water

1 bay leaf
4 to 6 ounces fresh sliced
  mushrooms
1 teaspoon Italian seasoning
1 onion, sliced
1 large size cooking bag

Brown roast in butter on all sides on top of stove. Season with salt and pepper. Put roast in cooking bag and sprinkle package of onion soup mix on and around roast. Add water, bay leaf, mushrooms, Italian seasoning and sliced onion. Cook in cooking bag in 350 degree oven for 2 hours.

Salisbury Venison Steak

1½ pounds ground venisonburger 1 (10 ounce) can golden
½ cup bread crumbs   mushroom soup
½ cup onion, chopped   2 cloves garlic, minced
½ teaspoon pepper   1 teaspoon salt
1 egg   1 teaspoon chili powder

Mix all ingredients and shape into patties (using only ¼ can of soup). Brown patties and add remaining soup mixed with ¼ can of water. Pour over patties and simmer 15 to 20 minutes.

Optional: Add one cup fresh sliced mushrooms before pouring over patties. Great over noodles or rice.

Honey Venison Bake

2 large venison steaks, about 2   ⅛ teaspoon freshly ground
   to 3 inches thick   pepper
½ cup flour   ½ teaspoon cayenne pepper
¼ pound butter   ½ teaspoon salt
3 cups sour cream (divided)   ¼ cup honey

Knead flour into steak, and brown it well in butter. Cover bottom of baking pan with 1½ cups sour cream. Add steak and seasonings. Pour honey over top. Cover and bake in 250 degree oven 1½ hours, or until tender. Add more sour cream, when necessary, to retain moistness. Add baked potatoes and your favorite vegetable side dish for a great meal.

Pot Roast Of Venison II

2½ to 3 pounds venison roast   ½ teaspoon dry sage
Salted water to cover   3 cups apple cider
2 cups water   2 carrots, sliced
2 onions, sliced   1 cup fresh mushrooms
½ cup sliced celery   2 cloves garlic, diced

Simmer meat in salted water to cover for 1½ hours. Drain and return to kettle with remaining ingredients. Cover and simmer until tender. Slice meat and arrange on hot platter to keep warm. Make gravy from cooking liquid. Serve with buttered noodles or rice.

Thanks, Dad, for this favorite restaurant recipe for what we call "Big Game Casserole" because ground elk, muledeer, moose, caribou, etc. could be substituted. Our family has enjoyed this venison meal since 1986. It is very easy to prepare and by changing the "cream of soup" you can change the dish considerably while it always turns out delicious.

Big-Game Casserole

1½ pounds venisonburger or
   sausage
1 cup chopped onion
1 teaspoon salt
½ teaspoon pepper
¼ cup butter

1 can condensed cream of
   mushroom soup
1 (7 ounce) package elbow
   macaroni
1 cup dairy sour cream
2 tablespoons white wine
1 (16 ounce) bag frozen sweet peas

In Dutch oven combine ground venison, onion, salt and pepper, then brown in butter. Stir in soup, cover, and simmer 10 minutes. Remove from heat. Meanwhile, cook macaroni according to package directions. Stir in sour cream, wine, macaroni, and peas into meat mixture. Pour into a 2½ quart casserole dish and bake in 350 degree oven for 35 minutes.

Spicy Venison Chili Burgers

1 pound ground venisonburger
2 pounds baking potatoes, peeled
   and cubed
3 tablespoons water
½ cup green onions, chopped
2½ tablespoons chili powder
¼ to ½ teaspoon cayenne pepper

½ teaspoon freshly ground
   black pepper
⅓ cup dry bread crumbs
2 tablespoons grated
   Parmesan cheese
Cooking spray

Preheat oven to 375 degrees. Cook potatoes in boiling water 15 minutes or until tender. Drain well, and mash; set aside. Combine 3 tablespoons water and green onions in a skillet; cook 4 minutes or until onions are soft and water evaporates. Combine onions, potatoes, venison, chili powder, cayenne pepper, and black pepper; stir well. Shape mixture into 8 patties. Combine bread crumbs and cheese; dredge burgers in mixture. Place patties on baking sheet coated with cooking spray. Bake at 375 degrees for 20 minutes, turning after 10 minutes.

The first time I enjoyed "Ella's Hunter Stew" was while deer hunting on the Arliss farm in upstate New York, probably twenty years ago. Our family has had it many times since thanks to Ella sharing her recipe with me. It is a crowd pleasing dish for any get-together. Thanks, Ella!

Ella's Hunter Stew

2 pounds venison roast or stew
  meat, cut in bite-size pieces
3 tablespoons olive oil
2 cloves garlic, minced
3 large onions, quartered
1 (6 ounce) can tomato paste
1 tablespoon flour
1 teaspoon chili powder
1 (16 ounce) jar chili sauce or
  salsa
1 teaspoon basil
1 teaspoon oregano

1½ tablespoons seasoned salt
1 (16 ounce) can stewed
  tomatoes
½ cup celery
½ cup parsley
1 cup water
3 medium carrots, sliced
½ pound elbow macaroni or
  small shells
½ cup shredded Parmesan
  cheese

In a large Dutch oven heat olive oil and brown venison cubes on all sides. Add garlic and onion and saute well, turning frequently. Stir in tomato paste, flour, chili powder, chili sauce or salsa, basil, oregano, seasoned salt, tomatoes, celery and parsley. Add water and simmer, covered, 1 hour and 15 minutes. Add carrots and simmer 45 minutes longer until carrots are tender. Meanwhile, cook elbow macaroni or shells, as package directs. Drain well, stir into stew, and mix in Parmesan cheese. So good!

Tasty Venison Heart

Dice up the heart and flour the pieces and fry in hot butter until brown in a fry pan that has lid to fit. Cover with water, season with garlic powder, salt and pepper to taste and simmer until heart is real tender.

Optional: Add one onion, sliced and 1 cup fresh mushrooms. More water or wine if liquid is needed.

Venison Chili

1 pound ground venison
1 tablespoon butter
1 small onion, minced
1 green pepper, chopped
1 large can chili beans or kidney
  beans
1 (16 ounce) can of stewed
  tomatoes
Salt and pepper to taste
2 teaspoons chili powder
1 (4 ounce) can mushrooms
Hot sauce to taste

In a large skillet with a lid, brown venison in butter, breaking the ground meat into small pieces as you brown it. Add onion and green pepper and cook until onion begins to brown, about 5 minutes. Stir often. Add beans, tomatoes, salt, pepper, chili powder, mushrooms, and enough hot sauce to suit your taste, stirring occasionally. Cook about 1 hour over medium heat. Make ahead of time. Reheated it is even better!

Mary, the mother of my hunting buddy, Mark, is a very good cook. After enjoying her "Venison Stroganoff" dish last deer season, I just had to have her recipe. Try it to see if you like it as much as I did. Good!

Mary's Venison Stroganoff

2 pounds venison steaks
1 teaspoon salt
1 teaspoon black pepper
½ cup flour
2 tablespoons butter
2 cups mushrooms, sliced
1 cup onions, chopped
2 cloves garlic, minced
1 cup green pepper, diced
3 tablespoons flour
2 tablespoons tomato paste
1 (16 ounce) can cold beef broth
2 cups dairy sour cream
3 tablespoons white wine

Cut venison into ¼ inch strips; dredge in salt, pepper, and flour, and brown quickly on all sides in Dutch oven in melted butter. Remove venison from Dutch oven. Add mushrooms, onions, garlic, and green pepper to the pan drippings. Cook 3 to 4 minutes until pepper and onion are barely tender. Blend in flour, tomato paste and beef broth. Stir mixture constantly until it thickens. Return venison to Dutch oven. Stir in sour cream and wine and cook through. Serve over rice or noodles.

Venisonburger Meatloaf

1½ pounds ground venison or venisonburger

2 slices bacon cut fine

1 teaspoon salt

1 cup carrots, grated or ground fine, raw

1 cup raw potatoes, grated or ground fine

1 small onion grated fine

1 small (3 or 4 ounce) can mushrooms and liquid

½ cup fine dry bread crumbs

1 teaspoon chili powder, optional, but delicious

2 eggs beaten lightly with ½ cup water

½ cup finely chopped celery

Combine and bake in loaf pan in moderate oven at 325 degrees until done (1½ to 2 hours). Delicious!

Venison Meatloaf

1 pound ground venison or venisonburger

2 eggs

2 tablespoons grated celery

⅓ cup grated onion

1 teaspoon sage

⅔ cup bread crumbs

¼ cup Parmesan cheese

2 tablespoons grated cheese

1 teaspoon salt

Dash black pepper

1 cup milk

Catsup, to spread on top of loaf

½ cup water

Add ground venison, eggs, and other ingredients (except catsup and water) soaked in milk in a large mixing bowl. Mix well. Shape into a loaf and spread catsup on top. Place in greased pan. Add approximately ½ cup water around loaf. Top loaf with Parmesan cheese, cover and bake in 350 degree oven for 1 hour.

When you have one and a half pounds of ground venison, and you want to do something different for a special meal — try this recipe called "Mexican Sausage." Guaranteed to please when used in any other recipe!

Mexican Sausage

1½ pounds ground venison
1½ pounds ground pork
1 medium onion, minced
2 cloves garlic, minced
1 to 2 tablespoons chili powder
1 teaspoon cumin (optional)

2 tablespoons red wine or wine vinegar
1 tablespoon paprika
2 teaspoons oregano
1 teaspoon parsley

Take ground venison and mix with 1½ pounds ground fatty pork. Combine with other seasonings and mix well. Roll into 3 one pound balls or loaves; place on freezer paper. Wrap each with plastic freezer wrap and drop into one quart freezer bags for quality freezer protection.

Try this ground sausage in place of ground venison sausage in your favorite chili recipe or pasta sauce.

Venison Salisbury Steakburgers
A hearty flavor to satisfy hungry hunters.

1½ pounds ground venisonburger
6 tablespoons steak sauce
½ teaspoon salt
¼ teaspoon pepper

1 (10½ ounce) can condensed onion or golden mushroom soup
½ cup catsup or chili sauce

In medium bowl, combine venison, 4 tablespoons steak sauce, salt and pepper. Shape into 4 burgers. In large skillet, brown burgers on both sides. In small bowl, combine remaining steak sauce, soup, and chili sauce or catsup. Pour over burgers. Simmer, covered 10 minutes or until meat is cooked as desired. Serve, garnished with sauteed mushrooms, if desired.

Venison With Hunter's Sauce

1½ to 2 pounds venison steak, cubed
4 tablespoons butter (divided)
2 medium onions, chopped
3 tomatoes, diced
6 large mushroom caps, sliced thin

1 teaspoon salt
1 teaspoon pepper
2 cloves garlic, diced
2 cups beef bouillon
2 tablespoons flour
¼ cup red wine or beer

Melt 2 tablespoons butter in a deep skillet and saute venison cubes and onions until transparent. Add tomatoes, mushrooms, salt, pepper and garlic. Blend in bouillon and simmer 1 hour, stirring occasionally. Meanwhile, blend the flour into 2 remaining tablespoons butter, creaming together well. Just before serving sauce, thicken with this flour-butter roux, add wine, blend well, and heat through.

We gave our artist friend, Jack Paluh (whose "In Thanksgiving" print is on the cover of our cookbook) this "Venison Jerky" recipe after sampling one piece...it was all over and he had to eat the whole bag that I gave him. "So good," he said.

Venison Jerky

3 pounds venison, cut into strip ½ to 1 inch wide
1 tablespoon vinegar
¼ teaspoon black pepper
½ teaspoon liquid smoke
¼ cup soy sauce

1 tablespoon steak sauce
½ teaspoon garlic powder
½ teaspoon onion salt
½ teaspoon hot pepper or Tabasco sauce

Soak venison strips overnight in refrigerator in the above combined ingredients. Drain and place on flat pan in oven so pieces do not overlap. Dry for 6 to 8 hours at 100 to 150 degrees or 4 to 5 hours at 180 to 200 degrees.

🔥 Seasoning Tip:

Sample your jerky when done. After placing jerky in a plastic bag or container with a lid, season it with black pepper, garlic powder or salt to taste. Add cayenne pepper to spice it up and store in refrigerator for a tasty snack. Bet you can't eat just one piece!

Bristol Pan-Fried Venison Steaks

1 pound venison steak, ½ inch thick
¼ cup cream or evaporated milk
¼ cup flour
½ teaspoon salt
½ teaspoon pepper
½ teaspoon garlic salt
3 tablespoons butter

Pound venison steaks thoroughly, if tenderizer is needed. Cut into serving pieces. Dip steaks into cream or milk, dredge in flour seasoned with salt, pepper, and garlic salt, and brown one side in hot butter. Turn. Can season with extra salt and pepper and garlic salt to taste. Continue cooking until second side is well browned. Venison steak is best eaten medium rare. Serve hot with baked potatoes.

In 1991 Pennsylvania Water & Woods magazine, cooking columnist Sharon Friend prepared our recipe "Stove Top Venison Stew" for her guests one weekend and it was a big hit. Later, she thanked us in an article in the magazine. True story. Enjoy!

Stove Top Venison Stew

2 pounds venison stew meat, trimmed and cubed
1 teaspoon salt
1 teaspoon black pepper
1½ cups flour
Cooking oil or butter
4 to 6 ounces fresh mushrooms, sliced
1 can cream of broccoli soup
1 teaspoon parsley
1 teaspoon marjoram
½ teaspoon onion powder
1 bay leaf
1 medium onion, sliced
½ teaspoon garlic powder

Salt and pepper your venison steak and dredge in flour. In a large skillet, brown the meat in oil. Add mushrooms and simmer a few minutes after browning. Add one can broccoli soup, a can of water and stir thoroughly. Then add this to steak and mushrooms and remaining seasoning from above. Simmer two hours stirring occasionally. Serve over mashed potatoes, rice or egg noodles. Serves 5 to 6.

Venison Steak
With Spicy Cheese Crumbs

1 to 1½ pounds venison steak,
  thinly sliced
1 cup cheese or spicy cheese
  crackers, crushed (your
  choice)
2 tablespoons grated Parmesan
  cheese
¼ teaspoon ground thyme

¼ teaspoon chili powder
½ teaspoon dried oregano,
  crushed
1 whole egg, lightly beaten
¼ to ½ teaspoon Tabasco sauce
3 tablespoons flour
½ teaspoon salt
⅛ teaspoon black pepper

Crush the crackers into fine crumbs by placing them in a heavy food-quality plastic bag, close and roll with a rolling pin. Combine the crumbs with the Parmesan, thyme, chili powder, and oregano. Spread on a plate. Mix together the egg and Tabasco; pour onto a plate. Combine flour, salt and pepper on a plate. Pat the venison with paper towels to absorb excess moisture. Dredge the venison in the flour, then in the egg, and then press a thick layer of the cracker crumbs onto all surfaces of the venison. Place on a plate and refrigerate 30 minutes for the crumbs to stick well.

Heat oven to 350 degrees. Spray a baking dish so as not to stick. Place venison in the dish and bake 35 to 45 minutes to medium rare-medium doneness.

Venison Cube Chili

1 pound venison, cut in ½ inch
  cubes
2 tablespoons olive oil
1 medium onion, chopped
Salt and pepper
2 to 4 tablespoons chili powder
½ teaspoon garlic powder
½ teaspoon oregano

½ teaspoon paprika
½ teaspoon cumin
Cayenne pepper to taste
3 tomatoes, chopped
1 (4 ounce) can mushrooms,
  drained
1 green pepper, chopped
2 cans chili beans

Barely cover the bottom of a 3 quart Dutch oven with olive oil. Brown onion and fry until slightly brown. Add venison and cook until tender, adding salt and pepper to taste. Add remaining spices, chopped tomatoes, mushrooms, green pepper, and chili beans. Cover and simmer for 60 minutes.

Bill's Venison Chili

1 pound venison meat, cubed or
  venison burger
1 onion, cut up
1 package Adolph's hot and
  spicy chili mix, to taste
2 cloves garlic, minced

2 (15 ounce) cans stewed
  tomatoes, crushed
2 (15 ounce) cans chili or kidney
  beans
1 small can crushed chives
1 can water

Cook venison with onion and drain. Add remainder of ingredients and cook for 1 hour, slowly. Serve with bread.

Dad first prepared this delicious venison dish for me many years ago. He did not have a name for it and had the seasoning amounts in his head until one day before enjoying the recipe again, I wrote down the ingredients as he prepared the dish. You will love "Saucy Dutch Oven Venison Steak."

Saucy Dutch Oven Venison Steak

1 to 1½ pounds venison boneless
  round steak, cut into bite-size
  serving pieces
¼ cup all purpose flour
1 tablespoon olive oil
1 large onion, chopped (about 1
  cup)
2 cloves garlic, diced
1 (16 ounce) can whole potatoes,
  drained (keep liquid)
½ cup catsup or chili sauce
1 tablespoon Worcestershire sauce

1 teaspoon hot pepper flakes
1 teaspoon instant beef bouillon
  or 1 cube
1 teaspoon salt
½ teaspoon dried marjoram
  leaves
½ teaspoon black pepper
1 (10 ounce) package frozen
  Italian green beans
1 (2 to 3 ounce) can sliced black
  olives

Coat venison steak pieces with flour. Press into venison. Brown venison in olive oil in Dutch oven. Push venison to side. Cook and stir onion and garlic in oil until tender; drain. Add enough water to reserved potato liquid to measure 1 cup. Mix potato liquid, catsup, Worcestershire sauce, pepper flakes, instant bouillon, salt, marjoram, and pepper; pour on venison. Heat to boiling; reduce heat. Cover Dutch oven and simmer until venison is tender, 1¼ to 1½ hours. Rinse frozen beans under running cold water to separate. Add potatoes, beans and olives to pan. Heat to boiling; reduce heat. Cover and simmer until beans are tender, 10 to 15 minutes more. Pass the Italian bread, please! Delicious!

Lane, a southern hunting partner who is mentioned in one of my deer tales, is the one who prepared this recipe for me at his home one evening before our deer hunt. "Easy Venison Stew" was a tasty dish and he was proud to share it with me. Thanks, Lane. Enjoy!

Easy Venison Stew

3 pounds venison stew meat, cubed
Salt, pepper and flour
3 slices bacon, diced to 1 inch
$^{1}/_{4}$ cup butter
$^{1}/_{4}$ cup water
$^{1}/_{2}$ tablespoon vinegar
$^{1}/_{4}$ cup red wine
$^{1}/_{2}$ cup celery
1 carrot
1 apple, chopped
$^{1}/_{2}$ tablespoon lemon juice

Use less tender cuts of venison. In a bag coat venison cubes with salt, pepper, and flour; saute venison and bacon in hot butter until well browned, turn frequently. Add water and vinegar, cover closely and cook until tender (2½ hours) adding more water as needed. ½ hour before meat is done add remaining ingredients. Cook until vegetables are done. Great with garlic bread.

Easy Venison Rump Roast

3 or 4 pound venison rump roast
1 teaspoon salt
1 teaspoon pepper
$^{1}/_{4}$ cup butter
4 tablespoons flour, or as needed
2 tablespoons soy sauce
2 tablespoons Worcestershire sauce
1½ cups water
1 bunch green onions, chopped
1 teaspoon garlic powder
1 teaspoon onion powder
1 teaspoon Italian seasoning

Sprinkle roast generously with seasoning, rub carefully with butter, generously, and sprinkle lightly with flour. Sear in 500 degree oven for 20 minutes, then turn oven down to 325 degrees. Place roast in a large cooking bag coating the bag with flour according to directions on box. Mix soy sauce, Worcestershire sauce, 2 tablespoons flour, and water and pour over the roast. Add the chopped green onions and seasonings. Roast in 325 degree oven for 2 hours. Gravy can be made from the drippings in the bag. Enjoy with baked potatoes.

Sweet And Sour Venison Pot Roast

3 to 4 pound venison rump roast
4 tablespoons butter (divided)
1 or 2 sliced onions
4 cloves garlic, diced
1 cup wine vinegar (or plain)

³/₄ cup brown sugar
¹/₂ teaspoon nutmeg (less if
    desired)
1 tablespoon parsley
1 teaspoon chili powder

In 2 tablespoons butter, cook onions and garlic in Dutch oven or large heavy kettle until transparent. Remove onions and garlic and save. In remaining butter, brown venison roast well on both sides. Add onions, garlic, vinegar, brown sugar, nutmeg, parsley and chili powder. Stir liquid around roast until well mixed. Cover tightly. Simmer 2 to 3 hours until meat is tender or put in 300 degree oven and cook for about 3 hours. If liquid is not thick enough when meat is removed, thicken with cornstarch for flavorful gravy.

*Optional use of your crock pot (4 to 6 hours) using same ingredients as above.

Hearty Pittsburgh Venison Stew

2 large onions, sliced
3 pound venison roast cut into
    1¹/₂ inch cubes
4 carrots, peeled and sliced
4 celery ribs, sliced
6 potatoes, cut into ¹/₃ inch thick
    slices

Salt and pepper, to taste
1 teaspoon dried Italian
    seasoning
2 cups beef broth
2 cups white or red wine
¹/₂ teaspoon chopped parsley

In a large pot, place a layer of the sliced onions, then the venison cubes, carrots, celery and potatoes. Season the layers with salt, pepper and Italian seasoning. Repeat the layers. Finish with potatoes as the top layer. Pour in just enough broth and wine to cover the layers. Bring stew to a boil. Lower the heat and cover pot. Let stew simmer for 2¹/₂ to 3 hours, or until tender. Stir occasionally and add more wine or broth, if needed. Top with parsley.

Serve in large soup bowls with Italian or French bread and butter.

The opening of deer season is only hours away. Just enough time to make a hearty venison stew for hungry hunters.

Pennsylvania Deer Camp Stew

1 pound bacon, chopped
1 bunch green onions, chopped
2 pounds onions, chopped
6 pounds venison, cubed
2 pounds boneless pork, cubed
$1/4$ cup Italian seasoning
1 tablespoon salt
1 tablespoon black pepper
1 small bottle Worcestershire
   sauce
1 small bottle Tabasco sauce
   (optional)

1 bunch celery, chopped
2 bell peppers, sliced
2 to 3 pounds potatoes,
   chopped
2 (10 ounce) packages frozen
   succotash
1 ($14^1/2$ ounce) can whole
   tomatoes
3 ($14^1/2$ ounce) cans stewed
   tomatoes
1 (10 ounce) package frozen
   peas and carrots

Brown bacon in Dutch oven. Remove bacon bits and set aside on foil covered with paper towel to drain. Pour half bacon grease into a second large Dutch oven. Chop green and white onions. Add cubed pork, venison and onions in equal amounts to both Dutch ovens.

Brown venison, pork and onions for 20 to 25 minutes or so. Add bacon and remaining seasonings and vegetables equally to each Dutch oven. Cook slowly for $1^1/2$ hours or until tender; stirring occasionally and add water as needed. Serve in bowls and pass the bread, please!

Venison Chinatown

1 pound venison, thinly sliced
3 cloves garlic, diced
$1/4$ teaspoon ground ginger
2 tablespoons dry sherry
1 tablespoon soy sauce

1 tablespoon cornstarch
1 tablespoon oil
1 ($14^1/2$ ounce) can stewed
   tomatoes
Hot cooked rice

Combine garlic, ginger, sherry and soy sauce; toss with venison. Stir in cornstarch; mix well. In hot skillet, cook meat in hot oil over high heat, stirring constantly until browned. Add tomatoes and cook over high heat until thickened, stirring frequently, about 6 minutes. Serve over hot rice.

Not long ago our family prepared this "Cheesy Venison and Vegetable Bake" recipe. It deliciously served five or six. It is a great casserole so give it a try.

Cheesy Venison And Vegetable Bake

1 pound venison steaks, thinly
    sliced or pierced
1/4 cup onions, chopped
1/2 cup sliced fresh mushrooms
1 (11 ounce) can cheese soup
1 (10 ounce) can evaporated milk
1 teaspoon salt
1 teaspoon Italian seasoning

1/2 teaspoon garlic powder
1/2 teaspoon black pepper
1 (12 ounce) package egg
    noodles or bow ties
1 (10 ounce) package frozen
    vegetables, thawed (lima
    beans, peas, or broccoli)
1 cup cheddar cheese

In a Dutch oven brown venison in 2 teaspoons butter or olive oil along with onions and mushrooms for 10 minutes or so. Add soup, milk, salt, Italian seasoning, garlic powder, and black pepper. Simmer for 10 to 15 minutes, stirring occasionally. Cook pasta according to package directions. Drain. In a three quart casserole dish place a layer of pasta along the bottom. (May use cooking spray to prevent sticking). Then put a layer of venison and veggies followed by a layer of noodles. Continue the layering process until done. Top with cheddar cheese and bake at 350 degrees for 45 minutes. Delicious family venison meal.

Deer Camp Sloppy Joes

Young cooks at camp or home will enjoy preparing this easy meal for friends.

1 pound venisonburger or
    sausage
1 (5 ounce) bottle of your
    favorite steak sauce
1 cup green onions, chopped

1 (15 ounce) can tomato sauce
1/4 cup chili or picante sauce
1/2 teaspoon garlic salt
1 garlic clove, diced
1/2 cup Parmesan or cheddar cheese

Brown your venison in a large frying pan until done, (10 minutes or so). Mix in steak sauce, onions, tomato and chili sauce, garlic salt and garlic. Simmer uncovered 15 to 20 minutes. Spoon venison sloppy joes over split hamburger buns and top with cheese.

Cooking Loder Family Favorite Venison Recipes

Over the years, for a variety of reasons, we have made recipe scrapbooks to keep track of favorite recipes/meals we shared, that were very tasty or even memorable. Each year there are favorites or reliable recipes we prepare again when the occasion arrives or we miss not having "that favorite dish in a while." That is what this section is made of and we hope you find these recipes to be tasty and memorable, too!

These recipes have been made to be new and improved for our preferred taste. We encourage you to add or change ingredients to suite your tastes for hotter, sweeter, more herbs, more garlic, etc. to suite your meal preference. Enjoy!

Steve's Yankee Style
Venison Casserole

1 pound venisonburger or
    venison sausage, browned
1 stalk celery, chopped
1 zucchini, sliced
1 summer squash, sliced
4 green onions, chopped
4 fresh mushrooms, sliced
1 large potato, sliced thin

1 tablespoon Worcestershire
    sauce
1 (14½ ounce) can beef broth
2 cloves garlic, diced
1 teaspoon onion salt
1 teaspoon black pepper
1 teaspoon chili powder
¾ cup cheddar cheese

Preheat oven to 350 degrees. After browning venisonburger, put half on bottom of 2½ quart casserole dish. Add half of the celery, zucchini, squash, onions, mushrooms, potatoes, Worcestershire sauce and beef broth. Put a layer of the remaining venison and again layer with remaining vegetables. Add garlic, onion salt, pepper, chili powder and remaining beef broth. Cover top with shredded cheddar cheese and bake for 1½ hours. Enjoy with garlic bread!

Cheesy Venison Rice Casserole

2 cups cooked rice
2 cups cooked, ground venison
1 (10 ounce) package cut
    asparagus
1 (10½ ounce) can cream of
    mushroom or cream of
    broccoli soup

2 garlic cloves, diced
1 small onion, chopped
¾ cup sour cream
4 sliced mushrooms
1 cup shredded cheddar and
    Monterey Jack cheese blend

Combine all ingredients and spoon into a 2-quart casserole dish prepared with vegetable spray. Cover and bake at 350 degrees for 20 to 30 minutes.

You just have to prepare the "Pittsburgh Venison Chowder" dish with some of your venisonburger or venison sausage. This might be just the recipe to use some of the Mexican Sausage you may have made up from one of our earlier recipes. It is an unusually nutritious and delicious chowder.

Pittsburgh Venison Chowder

1 tablespoon olive oil
1 pound venisonburger or
   sausage
1 large yellow onion, chopped
3 cloves garlic, minced
1 medium-size sweet green
   pepper, cored, seeded and
   sliced lengthwise into ¼ inch
   strips
1 (1 pound) can stewed
   tomatoes
1 (14¾ ounce) can beef broth

½ cup bottled clam juice
½ teaspoon dried basil,
   crumbled
½ teaspoon thyme, crumbled
½ teaspoon oregano, crumbled
½ teaspoon cayenne pepper
3 tablespoons minced fresh
   parsley (optional)
1 bay leaf
1 (6 to 7 ounce) can minced
   clams
1 (6 to 7 ounce) can shrimp

In a 4 quart Dutch oven heat olive oil over moderate heat; add venison, onion, garlic and green pepper and cook, stirring until venison is golden brown, about 15 minutes. Add tomatoes, broth, clam juice, dried basil, thyme, oregano, pepper, fresh parsley and bay leaf. Cover and simmer one hour. Add clams and shrimp to venison. Simmer, uncovered for 15 minutes. Discard bay leaf. Ah, so so good!

A DEER HUNTER'S WIFE KNOWS!
Deer season is "around the corner" when her husband will nightly wear camouflage boxers and tee shirts to bed. You know you are getting closer to the deer season opener when he starts telling about his dreams and about the deer that did or did not get away and why. 'Honey, have I heard this tale before,' I often ask?

Marinated Venison Loin Steak

2 pounds venison loin, cut into
   1 inch steaks
1 carrot, diced
½ cup cider vinegar
2 cloves garlic, crushed
½ teaspoon dry mustard
2 teaspoons prepared mustard
½ teaspoon salt
½ teaspoon chili powder
1 onion, chopped fine

1 teaspoon paprika
1 tablespoon lemon juice
1 bay leaf
4 tablespoons butter
¼ teaspoon Worcestershire
   sauce
½ teaspoon pepper
2 tablespoons tomato juice or
   catsup

Make marinade: Combine all ingredients except the venison, and bring slowly to a boil. Boil 5 minutes. Use to marinate venison steaks 6 hours in refrigerator. Remove steaks from marinade and sear on both sides in broiler under high heat. Reduce heat and broil, basting often with marinade until steaks are done to taste, 4 to 5 minutes per side. Serve with mushrooms sauteed in butter and parsley. Venison is at it's juicy best when pink in the middle. Like beef, it does not have to be cooked through like pork.

Barbecued Venison

1½ to 2 pounds venison,
   thawed and boneless
4 slices bacon, chopped
Barbecue Sauce:
½ cup water
2 medium onions, sliced
2 tablespoons brown sugar
⅛ cup lemon juice

¼ cup vinegar
¼ cup catsup
4 ounces tomato sauce
½ teaspoon garlic powder
½ teaspoon dried mustard
2 tablespoons Worcestershire
   sauce

Parboil venison in water, allowing about 10 minutes per pound. Mix barbecue sauce ingredients together and simmer for 10 minutes while venison is cooking. Add bacon to a Dutch oven or large frying pan, and saute parboiled venison on all sides. Add the Barbecue Sauce and simmer with venison over medium heat for at least an hour, or until tender. Serve over bread or rice.

This homemade "Old-Time Venison Sausage" recipe is our favorite by far. You will enjoy using it in special family recipes. Making it by hand and done right will take one person a couple of hours to make and freeze ten pounds of venison sausage, but it is well worth your effort. Enjoy!

Old-Time Venison Sausage

5 pounds ground venison
1 to 2 tablespoons sage
2 teaspoons thyme
1¾ teaspoons crushed red
    pepper
2 tablespoons fennel seeds
3 cloves garlic, minced

5 pounds ground pork butt
2 to 4 tablespoons salt
1 to 2 tablespoons freshly
    ground pepper
2 tablespoons onion flakes
2 tablespoons Italian seasoning

Grind your own venison from trimmed deer front shoulder. Do it yourself or have butcher grind it for you and give it back fresh. Stop at grocer and have them grind a 5+ pound pork butt roast up for you. You now have to mix ½ the venison with ½ ground pork and ½ seasonings. Then mix meat and seasonings of other half. Now mix each 5 pound pan thoroughly together to have total of 10 pounds venison sausage. Roll into 10 one pound balls or loaves onto freezer paper. Wrap each with plastic freezer wrap and drop into one quart freezer bags for quality freezer protection. Lean and tasty!

A DEER HUNTER'S WIFE KNOWS!
She is living with a family man who loves deer hunting and the outdoors when he hunts tirelessly until he has their year's venison supply in their freezer. But we want to encourage all deer hunters to hunt and share their venison bounty with friends, neighbors and the needy in their communities across the country. Check with your local Salvation Army and church area food banks to help out. They gladly take processed venison donations. Thank you, Lord, for the God given, renewable resource of the whitetail deer and all legal wild animals of the land and air that you have blessed the earth with.

Surely it is the first venison steak you traditionally sample after each successful deer hunt. Where do I find this memorable venison steak that does not need much aging to be tender? Reaching inside the deer's cavity you will find the 2 fillets on either side of the deer's backbone between the hind quarters. They are easily removed by hand with little help from your hunting knife.

Fried Venison Fillets

First cool these strips of the finest venison steak in the refrigerator to firm the meat a day or two till frying. Cut steaks into three quarter inch steak tidbits. Heat 2 tablespoons oil and butter in a frying pan over medium heat. Add tidbits of tenderloin, ½ teaspoon each of garlic and onion powder. Fry 5 minutes on each side while adding salt and pepper to taste.

Just before done (medium rare) add ½ cup sherry, red or white wine. Turn heat to high for a minute or two. Serve immediately because this is steak as good and good for you as it gets.

Dad's Venison Steak Tips

This is a venison lover's favorite! Be sure to trim all visible fat off the meat before preparing.

2 pounds venison steak, cut into 1 inch cubes	2 garlic cloves, minced
2 cups beef consomme	1 cup chopped green onions
½ cup rosé wine	2 tablespoons cornstarch
¼ cup white wine	¼ cup water
3 tablespoons soy sauce	4 cups hot cooked rice (optional)

Brown venison on all sides in a large Dutch oven. Add consomme, wine, soy sauce, garlic, and green onions. Heat to boiling. Reduce heat, cover, and simmer 1 hour, or until meat is tender. Blend cornstarch and water and stir gradually into the stew. Cook, stirring constantly, until gravy thickens and boils. Cook 1 minute more. Serve over rice or noodles or even potatoes. Ah!

We have Rog Arliss to thank for the enjoyment of eating this very tasty "Venison Wild Game Ragout" dish. He is fond of using tomato soup and tomato juice in many of his venison recipes. He says it is the acid in the tomatoes that further tenderizes rich tasting venison. Taste it and see!

Venison Wild Game Ragout

2 pounds venison steak
3 tablespoons olive oil
2 large onions, chopped
½ pound bacon, chopped
1 teaspoon parsley
1 can tomato soup, undiluted
2 teaspoons bourbon or red
  wine
1 tablespoon salt

5 garlic cloves, crushed
1 teaspoon curry powder
2 tablespoons Worcestershire
  sauce
1½ quarts water
¼ cup beer
¼ pound fresh mushrooms,
  sliced

Cut venison into cubes about 1½ inches square. Heat olive oil in large skillet and add venison, onions, garlic and bacon. Cook until all is richly browned, stirring frequently. Add all other ingredients except mushrooms; cover and simmer for 50 minutes. Add mushrooms and simmer 10 minutes more. Serve over noodles or rice.

Gale's Venison And Vegetable Risotto

1 pound ground venison,
   venisonburger or sausage
1 cup fresh mushrooms, sliced
2 tablespoons olive oil
1/2 cup sliced zucchini
1/2 cup chopped red bell pepper
1/2 cup chopped onion

1 teaspoon crushed basil
2 cloves garlic, minced
2 teaspoons butter
1 cup cooked brown rice
2 (14 1/2 ounce) cans beef broth
2 cups water
1/2 cup gated Parmesan or
   cheddar cheese

In 3 quart sauce pan or Dutch oven brown venison of your choice and mushrooms for 10 minutes in olive oil. Remove and set aside. Saute zucchini, pepper, onion, basil and garlic in butter for 5 minutes. Add venison, cooked rice, beef broth, and water; cook 15 minutes, covered. Add Parmesan cheese to pan, stir and serve in big bowls. Pass the Italian bread and butter, please. Enjoy!

Our Venison - Mushroom Soup

1 pound venison steak, cut into
   cubes
2 tablespoons butter (divided)
1 onion, finely chopped,
   (about 1/2 cup)
1 small sweet red pepper, finely
   chopped (about 1/2 cup)

1 cup uncooked regular long-
   grain rice
1 (14 1/2 ounce) can beef broth
1 (10 3/4 ounce) can condensed
   cream of mushroom soup
1/2 teaspoon black pepper
1/2 cup frozen lima beans

In a 3 quart saucepan over medium-high heat, in 1 tablespoon butter, cook venison until browned, stirring often. Remove; set aside. In same saucepan, add remaining butter. Reduce heat to medium; cook onion, pepper, and rice until rice is browned, stirring constantly. Stir in venison, broth, soup, pepper, and lima beans. Heat to boiling. Cover; cook 25 to 30 minutes, stirring occasionally.

If you have been particularly blessed with a bountiful deer season, you may want to use this special recipe for "Holiday Tradition Sausage Stuffed Venison" for one of your deer's entire hind quarters (except the shank and hock; save them for grinding or a slow cooker recipe). Based on our experience of a couple of holidays gone by, you will have a memorable meal for your whole family. Do not hesitate to halve this recipe. Depending on the weight and size of the venison hind quarter, you may need a turkey size cooking bag.

Holiday Tradition Sausage Stuffed Venison

8 to 10 pound hind quarter of venison
1 pound Italian hot or sweet link sausage
3 to 4 tablespoons flour
1 cup red wine (Burgundy or Rosé)
2 cups water
½ pound (at least) bacon

Inside seasonings:
1 teaspoon salt
1 teaspoon black pepper
3 cloves garlic, diced
1 cup green onions
Outside seasonings:
1 teaspoon salt
1 teaspoon black pepper
1 teaspoon Italian seasoning
1 teaspoon chili powder

Bone out an 8 to 10 pound hind quarter of venison. Save the shank and hock for stews, soups or jerky. Open up the venison roast to be able to place one pound of Italian hot or sweet link sausage inside. Season venison inside with salt, pepper, garlic and green onions.

Fold venison over and season outside with salt, pepper, Italian seasoning and chili powder.

Place venison in a turkey or large size roasting bag and then into a large roaster or baking dish. Add 3 to 4 tablespoons flour, 1 cup red wine, and 2 cups water. Cover venison roast with as much bacon needed to cover completely. Roast at 350 degrees for 3 hours. After removing roast from oven let it cool 30 minutes before removing it from bag. Carve in roasting pan and serve with drippings. Add stuffing and other favorite vegetable side dishes for a memorable meal. Sausage is delicious, too! As always, enjoy...

Our Italian Style Meatloaf

1 pound ground venison or venisonburger
1 (14½ ounce) can Italian-style stewed tomatoes
½ cup chopped onion
½ cup chopped green pepper
1 teaspoon Italian seasoning

½ pound hot Italian sausage or spicy bulk sausage
1 cup fresh bread crumbs or mushroom pieces and stems
½ teaspoon minced garlic
1 egg, beaten
½ cup Parmesan cheese

In large bowl, combine all ingredients except Parmesan cheese; mix well. Place in 4½ x 8 inch loaf pan. Sprinkle top of loaf with Parmesan cheese. Bake at 325 degrees for one and a half hours.

Venison liver is tender and has a mild calves liver flavor. My dad always soaked venison liver in salt water for three days, changing the water at least daily before making baked liver and onions, and freezing the other half. Here is my recipe!

Venison Liver
With Onions And Mushrooms

1 large or 2 medium onions, sliced
2 green onions, chopped
2 to 3 garlic cloves, diced
½ cup butter, melted
½ venison liver sliced ¼ inch thick

¼ to ½ cup flour
1 teaspoon salt
½ teaspoon black pepper
1 teaspoon Italian seasoning
2 to 3 ounce fresh sliced mushrooms
¼ cup white or red wine

Preheat your oven to 350 degrees. First chop and dice onions and garlic. Melt butter in microwave. Slice venison liver thin and dredge in flour seasoned with salt, pepper and Italian seasoning. (Use a bag to coat completely.) Pour half of the butter into a casserole dish; add half of the liver slices and half of the onions and garlic. Then repeat layer of liver slices and remaining onions and garlic. Top with sliced mushrooms. Pour remaining butter and wine over top of liver. Then bake at 350 degrees for one hour. Baked venison liver this way is easy to prepare and a tasty treat. If you like liver, you will like this dish.

Traditionally, while boning out a deer, I will save venison trimmings to make at least one (3 pound) recipe for venison jerky. While there are plenty of jerky recipes around from which to choose, just prior to deer season, I will use "Our Favorite Venison Jerky" recipe on that specially saved venison. The jerky goes with me on opening morning of the deer season. Who ever is hunting with me that day gets a bag of venison jerky on the way in to our stands. Talk about Good! Ask Mark, Jim, Rog, Rick, Larry, Lane, John Paul, Lamonte, or Greg to name a few...

Our Favorite Venison Jerky

3 pounds venison, cut of your choice
1 teaspoon dehydrated minced onion
1 teaspoon prepared mustard

1 teaspoon garlic, minced
1 teaspoon black pepper
1 teaspoon cayenne pepper
$\frac{1}{4}$ cup soy sauce
$\frac{1}{3}$ cup Worcestershire sauce

Start by cutting your venison in quarter inch strips. Put the venison in a flat glass baking dish. In a small bowl mix remaining marinade ingredients and pour over venison. Marinate 10+ hours or overnight in refrigerator. To prepare, pat venison dry on paper towels. Slow cook venison 5 to 6 hours at 180 to 200 degrees. Bake venison strips on pizza trays or broiler pans. Sample jerky when done and add salt or more cayenne pepper to taste. It is a little work but deliciously worth your efforts. Retail beef jerky costs over $20 a pound, and this venison jerky tastes better and is better for you.

A DEER HUNTER'S WIFE KNOWS!
Our Quality Venison cookbooks are more than just cookbooks...They are so special that you can curl up in a special chair and enjoy a learning experience or even get interested in preparing a special venison meal for family and friends. A hunter's venison is delicious and nutritious when properly handled from field to freezer and then to your dinner table. Thank you Lord for our bounty, and you will like reading our tales and stories, too...

When we lived in Memphis, Tennessee we quickly found out how popular barbecue beef or pork was everywhere. After a little research I was ready to test barbecuing some of our venison. The "Memphis-Style Barbecued Venison Loin" recipe on your quality cared for venison is sure to please one and all anytime and anyway you prepare it — baked or grilled. Thanks, Memphis for the idea.

Memphis-Style Barbecued Venison Loin

1½ pounds venison loin steaks
Barbecue Sauce:
1 stick butter
1 tablespoon sugar
½ teaspoon chili powder
½ teaspoon ground sage
2 garlic cloves, diced

½ cup catsup, salsa or picante
1½ tablespoons lemon juice
1 tablespoon Worcestershire
   sauce
1 teaspoon salt
1 tablespoon onion flakes

Add above barbecue sauce ingredients to sauce pan and simmer 10 to 15 minutes. Pour ½ into baking dish and place steaks on top. Cover the top of venison with remaining barbecue sauce and bake at 350 degrees for 30 to 35 minutes. Great tasting medium rare to medium doneness.

Optional: Grill it!! Make sauce, coat venison thoroughly in a pan; then marinate 2 to 4 hours in the refrigerator. Grill over coals or lava rock 8 to 10 minutes each side or to taste; basting occasionally with barbecue sauce. Great steaks!

Yankee Venison Chili Without Beans

This is a hot chili so adjust red pepper flakes to your taste.

2 pounds venison round steak,
cut in cubes
2 tablespoons olive oil
1 medium onion, chopped
2 stalks celery, chopped
3 cloves garlic, minced
3 tablespoons dried ground red
pepper
2 teaspoons red pepper flakes

1 (16 ounce) can stewed
tomatoes
1 cup picante sauce
1 teaspoon Italian seasoning
1 cup green onions, chopped
1 (7 ounce) can diced green chili
peppers, drained
1 tablespoon ground cumin
1 teaspoon ground oregano

Brown the venison in the oil. Add the onion, celery, and garlic and saute until soft, 10 to 15 minutes. Add the remaining ingredients and enough water to cover and simmer for about 2 to 3 hours or until the venison is tender. Add more water as necessary for desired thickness. Pass the Italian bread and butter, please enjoy!

Venison Ragout

A very tasty dish for hungry hunters or the whole family.

2 to 3 pounds venison, cut into
one-inch pieces
4 tablespoons olive oil
3/4 pound mushrooms; whole if
small, halved if larger
1/2 teaspoon garlic powder or
1 small clove garlic minced
1 medium onion, diced
1 (6 ounce) can tomato paste,
catsup, or chili sauce

1/2 cup beef stock or bouillon
(optional)
1/2 cup rosé wine
1 cup burgundy wine
3 tablespoons brandy or
bourbon
1 cup beer or water
4 tablespoons flour
1/4 teaspoon black pepper
2 bay leaves

Brown venison in hot olive oil in deep skillet or dutch oven. Remove venison and replace with mushrooms, garlic, and onions, browning them slightly while stirring. Remove from pan and put with venison.

Shut off heat under skillet and stir in tomato paste, catsup or chili sauce and beef stock. In a separate bowl mix wine, brandy, and beer with flour; stir, then add to skillet, heating just short of the boiling point. Now add venison, mushrooms, onions, garlic, black pepper and bay leaves back to skillet. Cover tightly and simmer on low for 1½ hours. Serve over large egg noodles or rice!

Venison Steak
With Peppers And Mushrooms

1 pound venison round steak,
    fat trimmed-removed
1/4 cup soy sauce
2 cloves garlic, minced
1/2 teaspoon ground ginger
1/4 cup olive oil
1 cup red or green peppers cut
    into 1 inch squares

5 to 6 fresh mushrooms, sliced
1 cup green onion, thinly sliced
2 stalks celery, thinly sliced
1 tablespoon cornstarch
1 cup water
2 tomatoes, cut into wedges, or
    1 (15 ounce) can crushed

With a very sharp knife cut venison across grain into thin strips, 1/8 inch thick. Combine soy sauce, garlic and ginger. Add venison; toss and set aside while preparing vegetables. Heat olive oil in large frying pan or wok. Add venison and toss over high heat until browned. Taste meat. If it is not tender, cover and simmer for 30 to 40 minutes over low heat. Turn heat up and add vegetables, except tomatoes. Toss until vegetables are tender crisp, about 10 minutes. Mix cornstarch with water; add to pan; stir and cook until thickened. Add tomatoes and heat through. Serve with baked potato or rice. Preparation and cooking time 90 minutes. But, this tasty dish is worth it...

Stove Top Venison Steak

2 to 3 pounds venison steak,
    cubed
3 tablespoons butter or
    margarine
1 cup chopped onion or green
    onion
2 large cloves garlic, minced

Dash celery salt
1/4 cup dry red wine
1/4 cup water
2 tablespoons soy sauce
1 cup sliced fresh mushrooms
1 tablespoon parsley

Brown venison steak cubes in butter along with onion, garlic, and celery salt. Add wine, water, soy sauce, sliced mushrooms, and parsley to pan, then simmer one hour or until tender. After 30 minutes check to see if pan needs 1/2 cup water. If so stir in 2 tablespoons flour to water and mix before adding to the pan. Makes great gravy this way. Delicious venison steak.

My long time friend and avid deer hunter, Rick, gave me some seasoning ideas earlier this year that led to my preparing this "Pittsburgh Venison Loin" dish. With quality cared for venison — aged carefully, trimmed of all fat, boned and double wrapped before it is frozen — this savory venison steak dish should be up there with your all time favorites. Prepare it and see for yourself.

Pittsburgh Venison Loin

1½ pound venison loin steak
Cooking Sauce:
½ cup butter or olive oil
1 teaspoon minced garlic or
   2 cloves fresh garlic, minced

½ teaspoon black pepper
1 tablespoon minced onion
2 tablespoon spicy mustard
¼ cup soy sauce, regular or
   light

After heating butter or olive oil add remaining sauce ingredients. Pour half the sauce in glass baking dish and add venison; Pour other half of sauce over loin. Now bake at 325 degrees for 35 to 40 minutes to medium rare. Add steak to serving platter and cover with delicious gravy. Guaranteed — Ah!!

Anniversary Venison Loin

So, so, good — Honest!

1½ pounds venison tenderloin,
   trimmed
¼ cup grape or strawberry jelly
1 tablespoon Worcestershire
   sauce

½ teaspoon garlic powder
½ cup butter
1 teaspoon salt
1 tablespoon soy sauce
½ teaspoon black pepper

Make Sauce: Place all ingredients (except venison) in a coffee cup and microwave for one minute to melt butter. Pour half of the sauce into bottom of glass baking dish. Lay venison loin steak in dish and cover with other half of the sauce.

Now just bake venison steak at 350 degrees for 35 to 45 minutes for medium rare to medium doneness. Remove steaks to serving dishes and spoon on plenty of sauce. A very tasty steak treat I do believe.

Serve with hot buttered baked potatoes and fresh asparagus with fresh buttered mushrooms. Enjoy!

The next occasion when it is necessary to prove your venison cooking expertise — or prove that venison is savory and delicious and not 'gamey' — try using either the "Anniversary Venison Loin" or "Venison in a Super Sauce" recipe. Although easy to prepare, you will be very pleased how great your venison steak tastes. Enjoy!

Venison
In A Super Sauce

1¼ to 1½ pounds venison steak
⅓ cup salsa
¼ cup vinegar
½ cup water
2 tablespoons sugar
1 tablespoon mustard
½ teaspoon black pepper
1½ teaspoons salt

¼ teaspoon cayenne pepper
1 slice lemon
1 onion, sliced
¼ cup butter
½ cup catsup
2 tablespoons Worcestershire
   sauce
1½ teaspoons liquid smoke

In a medium saucepan, combine salsa, vinegar, water, sugar, mustard, pepper, salt, cayenne, lemon, onion, and butter. Simmer, uncovered, 20 minutes, stirring occasionally. Add catsup, Worcestershire sauce, and liquid smoke; blend well. Bring to boiling. Remove from heat. Spray 9x13-inch baking dish with cooking spray. Put in ½ the sauce, then add venison. Add remaining sauce and bake at 350 degrees for 30 to 35 minutes for delicious medium rare venison. Even your wife will love venison prepared in this Super Sauce!

A DEER HUNTER'S WIFE KNOWS!
The tradition of the annual deer season is approaching when her husband awakens in the morning to tell her about the nice buck he took in a dream last night. Then I am quick to remind him, once again, that we do not eat the horns. It's OK to dream about taking a nice buck, but remember to take any legal deer that God lets you come across so our family, or the less fortunate people around us, can enjoy nutritious venison again this year.

Why Hunt?

The reasons people hunt are just as varied as the millions of people who participate. Whether it's for companionship or solitude, to commune or participate with nature, the challenges or tradition, or perhaps just a fondness for wild meat, hunting remains, as it should always remain, a personal choice.

"In a civilized and cultivated country, wild animals only continue to exist at all when preserved by sportsmen." President Theodore Roosevelt

"The point is that...Americans like to hunt and fish, that hunting fever is endemic in the race, and that the race is benefited by any incentive to get out into the open, and is being injured by the destruction of the incentive in this case. To combat this destruction is therefore a social issue." Aldo Leopold, premier conservationist and father of wildlife management

Dollars: From Hunters, for Wildlife

State Licenses, Tags and Permits

New York was the first state to require a hunting license in 1908. By 1928 every state was benefiting from a dedicated source of funding for the new science of wildlife management, totally supported by hunting licenses. In 1996, 15.2 million licensed hunters (figure does not include hunters under the age of 16, subsistence hunters, or those legally exempt from license requirements) contributed over $542 million to state fish and wildlife agencies. Combined with fishing license sales, that total exceeded $989 million. Since 1923, sales of state hunting licenses, tags and permits have provided more than $8 billion toward wildlife management, habitat acquisition and enhancement, conservation law enforcement, shooting range constructions and hunter education.

Federal Duck Stamps

Legislation authorizing the Federal Duck Stamp Program was passed in 1934. Since that time hunters have provided well over $500 million for wetland purchase and protection through this program, and by 1996 the duck stamp revenue reached $22.9 million per year. The preliminary report for 1997 lists the revenue as $23.7 million.

Federal Aid in Wildlife Restoration Act of 1937

Better known today as the Pittman-Robinson (P-R) Act, this law imposes an 11% excise tax on firearms and ammunition, an 11% excise tax on certain archery equipment, and a 10% tax on pistols and revolvers. The P-R Act was adopted with the strong backing of sportsmen in response to wildlife population declines caused in large part by land use effects on wildlife habitat. P-R funds support wildlife management, hunter education programs and shooting range development. In 1997 P-R funds totaled $165.8 million. Since its enactment sixty years ago, the P-R act has distributed over $3.2 billion to state fish and wildlife agencies.

Our Nation's Economy

The 1996 National Survey of Fishing, Hunting and Wildlife Associated Recreation reports that in 1996 hunting expenditures alone totaled $20.6 billion. Hunting equipment expenditures were $11.3 billion, trip-related expenses totaled $5.2 billion, and other expenses such as land leases, membership dues and licenses, totaled $4.1 billion. Hundreds of thousands of jobs throughout numerous industries in the United States depend upon these hunting-related expenditures every year.

Hunter Education, Shooting Ranges and Law Enforcement

Pittman-Robertson federal aid funds are distributed to all 50 states to provide hunter safety training and education. Allocations of funds are determined by the state's population. Since 1979 more than $400 million has been appropriated for this purpose, with $28.8 million apportioned in 1997. Combined with state funds, this money supports the training of approximately 750,000 hunters each year, and over 20 million hunters to date. Every year more than 50,000 hunters donate $25 million worth of services as volunteer hunter education instructors.

The results of this training are remarkable. In the last 30 years the national hunting accident rate has decreased steadily with some states reporting as much as a 75% decline. By 1996 the U.S. accident rate was down to a low 6.12 accidents per 100,000 hunters, and the fatal accident rate had dropped to only .57 per 100,000. To help put this into perspective, the 1995 swimming accident rate as 218 per 100,000 swimmers, and based on estimates by the National Safety Council the fatal accident rate was 2.44 per 100,000 swimmers.

Hunters are still the strongest supporters of conservation law enforcement. In addition to license fees, hunters contribute to this important cause in many cooperative efforts. Perhaps most noteworthy in recent years are the various special programs such as Turn In Poachers and Operation Game Thief. In most states hunters initiated these systems, served on advisory committees and sponsored fund-raising activities.

The NRA and Hunting

The National Rifle Association of America was founded in New York in 1871 "for the improvement of its members in marksmanship." From this modest beginning, the NRA has evolved into a nationwide, nonprofit organization with a membership in the millions. Today, the NRA is a nationwide educational recreational and public service organization dedicated to the rights of responsible citizens to own and use firearms for recreation and defense.

The NRA has long recognized the importance of hunters in its fight to protect our right to keep and bear arms. Because hunters comprise a vast segment of the gun-owning public, the image they project reflects on all gun owners. The NRA has worked to promote safe and responsible conduct by hunters in the field since its beginning more than a century ago.

The NRA believes that well managed hunting is a beneficial use of renewable wildlife resources, which when left to nature, are lost to predation, disease, starvation or old age. Proper hunting is in complete accord with the moral tenets and historical facts of human existence. The hunting heritage predates recorded history by many centuries. The hunter's participation in the chase today is a healthy exercise, both physically and spiritually.

The hunter's interest in wildlife has been the principal factor in fostering sound management and conservation practices. The commitment of hunters and the funds they provide through special taxes and licenses safeguards the future of all wildlife species. Hunting is dominant among American traditions and has contributed substantially to our strong national character. Its future is a primary concern of the NRA.

Landowner Relations and Hunting Ethics

Each year thousands of acres of private land are closed to hunting. Unfortunately, it's because someone treated the land or its owners with disrespect.

You can improve hunter/landowner relations by getting permission before hunting on any property. Approach the landowner with courtesy; you'll have a better chance of getting permission and you can promote the image of the responsible hunter. Use a written permission form when seeking access to hunt.

All sportsmen and women have a responsibility to other hunters and landowners, the public, wildlife, and above all, to themselves. It is essential that all hunters abide by a code of ethics. Listed below is the NRA Hunter's Code of Ethics.

1. I will consider myself an invited guest of the landowner, seeking his permission, and so conducting myself that I may be welcome in the future.

2. I will obey the rules of safe gun handling and will courteously but firmly insist that others who hunt with me do the same.

3. I will obey all game laws and regulations; and will insist that my companions do likewise.

4. I will do my best to acquire those marksmanship and hunting skills, which ensure clean, sportsmanlike kills.

5. I will support conservation efforts, which can assure good hunting for future generations of Americans.

6. I will pass along to young hunters the attitudes and skills essential to a true outdoor sportsman.

Please abide by this code of ethics and help ensure our tradition is passed on to future generations for years to come. To join the NRA today, or for additional information regarding membership, please call (800) 672-3888.

National Rifle Association of America
Hunter Services Department
11250 Waples Mill Road
Fairfax, VA 22030
http://www.nra.org

Homespun Deer Tales

Early Outdoor Memories—
A Special Place

The deer tales to follow are true and are from the hunters journal that I began writing ten years ago. The tales begin with my early outdoor memories when growing up in the Finger Lakes area of upstate New York in the 1950s and 1960s. When I was fourteen years old, my uncle was the first to encourage me to hunt by letting me borrow his 12-gauge double barrel shotgun. That was all the encouragement I needed, and I have been hunting ever since.

While I was using my hunters journal to recreate these deer tales in story form for your reading pleasure, many fond memories of the people, friends, places and the delicious venison meals we have enjoyed over the years because of my being a deer hunter, came to mind.

Never before had I realized what an importance my deer hunting tradition has meant to my family. It is enough to make us stop and wonder what our lives would have been like had I not had a love of the outdoors and the deer hunting hobby I found there.

The good Lord willing, I will have many more years of deer hunting and there will be even more memories in the years to come. That will mean there will be more deer tales to share with you in our next venison cookbook. It is my hope that you enjoy reading these deer tales almost as much as you enjoy using our tasty venison recipes.

Early Outdoor Memories

As a kid growing up I spent most of my time, especially during the fall and winter, wandering the woods near my home in upstate New York. I eventually got a bee-bee gun and then my first 22 rifle. When I was old enough I hunted woodchucks and small game with the guys that I grew up with. Like most of our group after high school, we continued hunting deer, small game and waterfowl. We would often bring whatever game we had taken plenty of after a particular hunt into my father's restaurant for his approval. Often Dad said he had time to cook it if we dressed the game for him and that is what we did.

I do not know how many memorable game dishes we had that Dad prepared for us and other restaurant guests over the years. Eventually, there would come a time when I would have to learn to cook those game dishes for my family and friends to enjoy. Been there and done that — and I enjoy preparing game, especially venison, as much as I like to hunt it.

The Unforgetable First Buck

As fortune would have it I took my first deer before leaving for the Air Force in December, 1968. It was a nice sized deer with a small eight-point rack. Want to see a picture?

Here is the story....My dad had arranged for me to hunt with a friend of his from the restaurant on opening morning. So after breakfast at Dad's, we left in Francis Murry's pick-up truck. Francis put me out on watch before daylight just off a logging trail where two deer trails crossed. He told me to be quiet and do not move around more than necessary. He would come back for me at lunch time.

There was a lot of shotgun fire all morning but I did not see a deer. When Francis returned for me he was a welcome sight after

sitting for five hours in 15 to 20 degree temperatures. What you do when you are young!

We were driving along a logging road planning to get a bite to eat when I spotted a buck in the woods eating what looked like apples off an old apple tree. The buck just stood there as we got out of the truck to load deer slugs into our shotguns. I aimed for the buck's heart and lung area and fired first. The buck ran only twenty yards and collapsed. Luckily it was a heart shot and the buck was mine.

Three weeks later I was in the Air Force and Dad had my venison. Darn!

A Special Place

It must be twenty-five years ago now that I first began deer hunting on the Arliss family farm in Clyde, New York. I can remember the brothers talking to the newly invited guests about gun handling safety and the general do's and don'ts of how the hunting party will hunt together that day.

New hunting guests are encouraged also to aim carefully; to take one first and fatal shot at the deer presenting you with a shot. One well placed shotgun slug in a deer's lungs, neck, shoulder area will go a long way toward putting venison in everyone's family freezer and there won't be 5 or 10 or 15 deer wounded and lost at the end of each season. For over twenty-five years I have used this hunting advice and it has served me well.

It is only fitting here to thank Bill and Ella Arliss for their years of hospitality, friendship and excellent deer hunting. In particular, Ella, thanks for all your delicious venison cooking you have done for me and all our crew over the years. Thanks for your sense of humor, too. You always had more deer stories than the rest of us. Wishing you both all God's best.

My First Game Dinner

After going off to college a number of us were dedicated enough to do what it would take to continue hunting together each fall and winter. With the deer and waterfowl hunting continuing to improve we were taking more game than Dad had the opportunity to cook for us.

So, being forced to a tight budget because of college related expenses, I was not about to waste any future game meals. Ah, what to do? My girlfriend then — and now my wife Gale — had the answer. She went out and bought me my first game cookbook in 1973. I used it to previously prepare my first game dinner. The venison dish turned out delicious so I filled our freezer with game nearly every year since. Now I enjoy cooking as much as hunting, I think.

Today my wife likes not having to buy much meat for our home. Since I love game cooking, she does not have to cook many of our game meals either. So my wife sees my hunting trips in a different way than many hunter's wives do. Life is good!

The One Shot Buck

I returned home to upstate New York to attend college after serving four years in the Air Force and my friends in the Arliss Family welcomed me back to continue our deer hunting tradition.

Since I was not able to hunt much in the military, I was really excited when the opening Monday of the shotgun only deer season came in 1972. The hunting crew was larger and some of their names changed in the four years I was away. But the storytelling, kidding and joking was still in the air as we left the barn that opening morning before daylight.

It seemed like everyone had their favorite spot picked out to sit on watch until lunch time. Rog Arliss, my best friend from high school said, "Don't worry, come with me because I have a good

spot for you over near me." That morning there was shotgun fire ringing out near and far, but by lunch time neither Rog nor I had seen a buck. Two does got by Rog but no harm done.

Back at the farm house Mrs. Arliss (Ella) had plenty of last year's venison dishes prepared for the dozen or so hungry hunters. The only guys talking over lunch were the two guys I did not know, but who had fortunately taken their bucks that morning. They would be two of our primary drivers that afternoon on the three separate drives that were being planned.

One more buck was taken on that afternoon of deer drives. Larry Arliss, Roger's younger brother, has been a good shot for years. He took this nice six-point buck with one 12 gauge slug through the lungs while running in the woods. It went down about seventy yards away no less. I heard Rog congratulate Larry on a nice shot and Larry acted humble like it was nothing — just routine.

Although only does were spotted during our usual two hours of watch from ground stands that afternoon, most all agreed they would be back for more deer hunting in the morning. With a storm coming deer would move tonight and they could be anywhere tomorrow morning.

The next morning I was up and gone by 5:30 a.m. and met Rog and Larry at the farm for coffee and tips on where to sit on watch for my buck that morning. Since some snow had fallen overnight, it would help us in seeing and, if necessary tracking deer. It could be a big help.

Rog, Larry and I hunted on watch near each other that morning. At lunch time when we got back together only I had even seen a deer and I had to let two does pass because I did not have a New York doe permit.

We took our lunch break and rested up before listening to suggestions from the crew as to the best way to drive deer from the farm's four or five woodlots to the waiting watchers. Wind direction and possibly flooded timber weighed into the decisions.

The talk and anticipation had me excited even if it meant facing 20 degree weather again for four hours.

The Arliss family members managed the rotation of the hunting crew members between standers and drivers so everyone contributed fairly to our organized team hunting approach. Safety was always mentioned where and when appropriate. No deer was worth any kind of shooting injury.

Off we went in two pick-up trucks rested and excited. On the first one hour drive I saw deer ahead of me but did not see one with horns and did not shoot. Later there was some shooting as those deer or possibly others I had not seen on drive passed our watchers. When we drivers met our sitters or watchers, we learned six deer came by and Tom had missed a four-point buck. We rotated sitters and drivers. I was a watcher on the next drive.

The truck took us down the farm road and positioned us at the end of their woods that overlooked a pasture lot. Everyone was in hunter red and near trees for safety as usual. I was excited knowing the four-point buck that Tom had missed would likely be driven out of the woods and I could possibly get a shot. It would be the first buck for me in four years.

After hearing some intermittent shooting by the drivers, I did not know what to think. Suddenly, three deer came out of the woods to cross the pasture. They were doe, but not far behind was a buck. The three does were coming in my direction with the buck following. When in range I took off the shotgun's safety and slipped from behind the tree. The deer scattered, but I found the buck and fired at its shoulder. The buck went down and never moved. Hey, my first one shot buck!

A Hail Mary Six Point Buck

After fortunately being able to tag a four-point buck the year before on the Arliss farm, I was anxious to take several days off from college to hunt deer in the 1973 season.

The family was seeing enough deer that they were beginning to see areas of crop damage to their corn and alfalfa. During the waterfowl season hunts they encouraged me to again join their deer hunting crew. Hey, the venison from last year's buck meant many delicious meals to me over the past year. No problem, I will be back.

The opening of the southern zone of New York State's shotgun only deer season always opens on the third Monday in November. We had already experienced some cold weather and two significant snow falls. So opening morning was clear with a temperature in the teens. The snow was hard packed and crunchy as I made my way into the barn to meet our hunting crew. Bill Arliss, Ella's husband, and Rog and Larry's dad were mentioning they had been seeing deer crossing the large cornfield behind their house nearly every morning lately. He suggested two of us take up our morning watches along the west end of the cornfield just inside the woods.

I volunteered after Roger agreed that is as good a spot as any for me. Chip said he wanted to watch nearby, too. Off we went in the dark to Chip's truck. At 6:15 a.m. we were walking quietly down a farm road along the cornfield. Chip set up about half way down and I went down to the corner of the field and into the woods. The wind was blowing the trees real good shortly after sunrise. Between the sound of wind blown branches and flocks of duck and geese I surely would not hear deer moving through the woods near me on the way to the cornfield. So I had to carefully watch ahead and behind me.

Continually scanning the field edge for deer movement kept me alert for an hour or so, but then the cold wind was becoming a distraction. Then, two deer quickly entered the cornfield out of range to me but close enough for Chip to shoot if there was a buck trailing them. Wow, I wished I was closer. I was not cold anymore. Maybe ten minutes later a buck comes out of the woods and starts to cross the cornfield. I keep waiting for Chip to shoot. The buck could have run off but Chip finally fired his Browning shotgun. His first shot missed, but the second downed the buck.

Later I met up with Chip to help him get the deer on to his four-wheeler. He'd take it to the truck and back up to the barn. Being excited I chose to stay on watch until lunch when he'd return for me. Not another deer came out of the woods to cross the cornfield for hours. When I was disappointed enough, and cold enough that I had to move, I found a better tree to shield me from the wind. Finally Roger came back for me, but I was nearly frozen to that tree.

Ella Arliss had baked a huge tray of venison steak and onions as well as venison stew for all the hunters to enjoy. Man, I needed some warm nourishment to warm me up. I was not alone in being cold. I learned some of the crew took the cold better than others.

After lunch and a brief rest the plans were being made for two deer drives behind the farmhouse. Later we would all pick a spot to hopefully ambush our buck while on watch before sunset. As luck would have it, I would be a watcher on the first drive down toward the camp. I would be watching for a buck crossing the pasture where I took the four-point the year before so I was excited.

We watchers were dropped off first and we moved into a safe position where the drivers would be pushing the deer to us. Not knowing where a buck would exit the woods ahead of the drivers means each watcher has a fair chance at getting their buck if the drivers do not get it first. Drivers get there share of bucks too, season in and season out.

The sound of several slugs going off startled me. The drivers were closer than I thought. Wow, would I get a good shot at my buck. Relax, I thought, and just then four doe suddenly were bounding across the pasture away from me. I look back at the field line again and a buck comes out in high gear. When I have a clear shot in range I shoot once, twice, then my last slug. Clean misses — so I find another slug in my pocket, chamber it, find the deer on the other side of the field going away from me; I take careful aim and fire and the buck crumbled. I got out another shell, chambered and aimed to shoot again if the deer got up. It never moved for five minutes. It was only then that I noticed how far away the deer had

dropped. When a couple of our drivers met up with me, they asked if I got the buck. I said, "Yes." "Where is he?" "down over there by the tree line." "You're kidding!" "No..."

They walked with me over to the buck and it was 170 long paces to the six-point buck. We could not see where the buck had been hit to bring it down. Finally Rog noticed the slug hit the buck in the back of the head. It died of more of a concussion than a shotgun slug wound.

You have heard of the desperation pass or Hail Mary pass for a touchdown in football. This has to be the Hail Mary shot of my deer hunting career to this day! Thanks, Lord, for the great eating venison.

A Deer Hunting Memory
It Does Not Get Any Better Than This

In 1975 I was in my senior year of college. Our deer hunting on the Arliss dairy farm seemed to be slowly improving in each of the three prior seasons. Naturally I hoped that this season I would again be blessed with taking a nice buck. By now, my only venison cookbook had me cooking up delicious, nutritious venison meals for one and all. Is it any wonder while duck hunting in October I was dreaming about deer hunting next month.

Due to college class requirements I could only take the first day of this deer season off. Other than that I would hope to take a buck on one of the only two Saturdays of the short season. When I met with Bill, Ella and their sons the weekend before the Monday opener, they all agreed they were seeing more bucks than usual this year. The weather had been unusually warm so comfortable deer hunting would be a nice change for opening day.

Rog called on Sunday and said he had found a great place for the two of us to hunt on the farm opening day, but it meant I had to get to his house at five a.m. and bring a lunch because we had a

long way to go to get into position for our day of deer hunting. I know Rog and trust his judgement regarding deer hunting decisions on the farm, especially, so I did not question him. "Rog, I will be at your house at five a.m."

I awoke at 4:00 a.m. and was at Rog's house before 5:00 a.m. As expected he is up and ready. The plan is to walk deep in a piece of their property called 'The Triangle" because of its shape. We would use flashlights to get us through the swamp and woods so we could be on watch 150 yards apart an hour before sunlight. The reason for this was Rog understood a farm near his that was not normally hunted was going to be hunted opening day. Rog figured bucks might slip through their crew and cross his property via the triangle.

Rog dropped me off on watch and said he would come for me if he gets a buck or before dark whichever comes first. That would make this a long day, but it was warm and comfortable soon after the sun came up. I thought this is a great plan so I hoped at least one of us gets his buck.

With daylight coming the shotguns firing could be heard near and far. Silently I noticed deer movement in front of me at about eighty yards. It looked like four doe from what I could see. Knowing a buck can at times trail does I hoped a buck was soon to follow — but no luck. Maybe an hour after the four doe passed me from right to left at 70 yards distant, some does were now on the same path coming back from left to right. I raised my 12 gauge shotgun, took off the safety, and followed the deer one by one to within range.

So as not to hit brush I like to aim into a clearing that the deer I want pass through. It all happened in three seconds just like this: The first deer in the clearing is a doe, second a doe, third a doe, fourth spike horn, aim and shoot at a vital area. The buck went down and never moved. At 7:30 a.m. I had taken a nice sized spike buck with one shot. It was a sunny, fall-like day. With my buck dressed and tagged it really was a beautiful day to be in the woods. Some great eating venison this year!

The shotgun firing continued on and off all morning. I thought of dragging my buck to the road we came in on, but was not sure how far it was and I did not want to wander off in the wrong direction so I gave thanks and waited.

As our good fortune would have it, around noon there was shooting near us. Then the sound of water splashing. It must be deer racing across the stream in Roger's direction. Then one boom and silence. I never saw the deer. About an hour later I was thinking, "I hope Rog got his buck." Not long after that I can see Rog coming through the woods toward me. He is moving slowly. Hey, he must have his buck. I went to help him bring it over to mine and we shared my bag lunch. We had to swap stories on how we each made the one vital shot.

I remember dragging those two bucks out of a swampy woods was NO easy task. Rog will agree with me 100% knowing we will enjoy eating nutritious, delicious venison all year makes the dragging chore a little easier, until the next time. Thanks, Lord!

One Very Important 6-Point Buck

Just before the 1979 Virginia gun deer season I was laid off from my job almost without warning. My wife was not working because she was at home caring for our one year old daughter.

After several weeks unemployment started coming in and we, also, had some savings to help our budget. Since most of our savings was in the house we had purchased just six months earlier, we could see financial problems ahead if I did not find work.

When the deer season arrived, I convinced my wife to use some of our money to buy my big game license and several tanks of gas. We could at least eat well if I could manage to take a buck.

The only place I had permission to hunt was on a neighbor's farm 60 miles from our home in Roanoke, Virginia. Over the two week season I hunted all day every other day with my 12 gauge shotgun. Despite lots of prayer for determination I was about to

give up the cause because of the expense of gas, cold weather and loneliness my hunting quest had caused.

Thank you, Lord, for helping me one last time on the last day of the season. The story goes something like this. Up at 4:30 a.m. and on watch near a buck scrape line around 6:30 a.m. As daylight slowly came I remember praying for God's blessing on me for a buck. My wife wanted the 40 to 50 pounds of nutritious, savory venison for our family as much as I did. Knowing this made me tough out one last day's hunt.

When the sun rose, the day was clear and crisp with the mountain temperature at 15 to 17 degrees. I was as quiet and still as I could be watching that trail for the first two hours, but gradually I began to shiver. By 8:30 a.m., thinking I can't take this cold much longer, I saw a movement through the trees. When I saw horns, I raised my three shot Winchester shotgun loaded with one #4 buck shot and two deer slugs.

At 20 yards I fired the buckshot at the deer's neck as it stared at me. Boom — It ran off so I aimed and fired again and again at its front shoulder area. The deer kept running until it was out of sight. I was excited and mad at myself because my buck should be on the ground. I had my chance.

After a five or ten minute wait, I had to get on what I hoped would be the buck's blood trail. Not far from my first shot I found blood and lots of it down the trail. When I found my buck 100 yards from where we 'first met', I was just ecstatic. I thanked Jesus. Talk about happy. It was an effortless deer drag to the car. Gale will call me a hero. Ah, life is good this day!

The Lucky Tree Stand Buck

In August of 1980 I took a promotion that would bring us to Bristol, Virginia-Tennessee to live. I talked hunting with my customers and at sporting goods stores and was able to find some small and big game hunting in the area.

Over the winter I got involved with Ducks Unlimited and continued trying to meet guys who hunt. Then, Fall of 1981 I met a customer, Jack Washburn, who had a little land that I could deer hunt only.

The opening week of the 1981 deer season found me in the Sales Management seminar in Roanoke, Virginia. That first Saturday afternoon home I went out to hunt Jack's land. I did not see a deer but met up with a guy who told me to hunt the top of the ridge in the early morning because he had missed a six-point buck there opening day five days earlier.

O.K., Monday I took a vacation day and went and hunted that ridge alone. Since I had Jack's permission to hunt his land, I told another hunter who was in a tree stand on the ridge that I was given permission to hunt there all day. I meant for him to know I had permission to hunt on the property and hunt safely. He must have been trespassing because he got out of the stand and let me have it. Time was 7:00 a.m. and the sun is just coming up. It is clear and mild around 30 degrees.

About 8:15 a.m. I spotted a buck coming along a trail toward my stand. But he saw me move and turned off the trail. I didn't have time to think and I lowered my Winchester 1400 12 gauge automatic and fired. The deer went down, but was still alive. I thought about trying a finishing shot but it got up and ran off before I could shoot.

I nervously waited 10 minutes and then had to get down to see how much blood was around the area where he went down. He was hit pretty good and in the distance I could hear it breathing loudly. A lung shot for sure! I would have sat down and waited for the deer to breathe its last, but I was too nervous and excited so I cautiously stalked the deer for a finishing shot. Wrong!

When I spotted the deer in the brush 50 yards away it was laying down. I put my quick point scope on it and fired. When the buck got up and ran, I nearly dropped my gun! But I managed to follow the deer running through the brush and fired my third and

last deer slug. I went to where I shot at the buck laying down and there wasn't any blood on the ground or in the direction where it ran. I was shocked! I could not have missed. After a few minutes I began to make circles around the area where the deer last fell and the direction it ran. I found the six-point buck not 25 yards from where I shot at it laying on the ground! Looks like the first slug hit on the right side just below and in back of the heart. It got a little of its lung. The second shot was another shoulder shot and the last running through the brush slug — a Hail Mary — got the deer in the neck breaking the vertebrae or spine.

That was a beautiful morning to be in the woods — sun shining, +30 degrees, could see for miles. But when dragging the buck out I injured my lower back muscle that I had hurt years ago playing football. What a difficult time getting him out alone to the car with a pulled back muscle. Determination!!

That deer was good eating, I'll tell you. Thank you, Lord, for the venison for my family.

A Buck's Costly Curiosity Costs Him

Late in November of 1983, the Tennessee deer gun season was drawing to a close and neither Dan nor I had even fired a shot at our buck. Despite the cold weather and occasional small snow fall, we had hunted hard, only to be disappointed.

This coming Saturday was going to be the end of the season and we were about out of good places to hunt. Wednesday night Dan called me to say he remembered he had hunted with a guy once in east Tennessee who had a farm with deer on it. He had found his phone number and had given him a call to see if we could hunt with him on this last Saturday. Sho-nuff (Tennessee talk) we were welcomed and we could even spend Friday night bunked in a small cabin back in the woods. Sounds good to me, I told Dan.

Dan picked me up about six p.m. Friday night and we loaded my gear into his covered pick-up. We drove about three hours

before reaching the farm. It had snowed off and on and we were hoping for a fresh snowfall overnight. It would make our hunting easier for tracking and trailing if necessary to find a possibly wounded buck the next day.

As expected a cabin it was. Bud, the owner, informed us, "no heat, no inside plumbing and no women." We laughed then, but it got down to near 10 degrees that night. We thanked God for good sleeping bags for sure.

Bud was a farmer in his early fifties who inherited the farm from his father after he had passed away three years before. He liked our company because we socialized and swapped deer tales until nearly midnight. Bud had given us his suggestions as to where he felt we were most likely to get a shot at a buck the next day. It was near midnight when Bud left for his warm home some eighteen miles away.

Dan and I were up at five a.m. We both knew we did not want our families to go without savory, nutritious venison dishes for next year so it was take a buck now or never. After getting dressed in what felt like a 20 degree cabin, we drank some coffee, stuffed our pockets with candy bars and sandwiches and headed to the truck carrying our shotguns and deer slugs.

The ground was rock hard and with a stiff breeze from the north I did not want to think of how cold it was. We drove the farm road Bud had told us about until it ended. The plan was for Dan to hunt the woods on one side of this pasture and I was to take a stand on the other side in the woods. We agreed not to move far from our original stand locations in case either one of us needed the other to help get a buck out to the truck! I left Dan and with my shotgun and flashlight in hand, I headed into the darkness toward my ground watch.

I stayed just inside the woods when I found them and when daylight would come, I would do some still hunting. Eventually, I would set up a tree seat in an area where deer sign was plentiful and sit on watch for my buck. Your chances of taking a buck are

much greater if you are sitting motionless when a buck moves into view.

As cold as I was and pray as I might to see a buck that morning, I never saw a deer. It was around 11:30 a.m. when cold and discouraged I started slowly making my way toward the truck. Since the truck was open I got in out of the wind and started it before hitting the horn hard several times. Dan would be back soon.

When I saw Dan coming I got out of the truck to talk to him. I heard a dog barking as Dan was trying to answer my question. I told Dan "maybe that dog is on a deer." I could hear the dog coming closer to the field edge as Dan neared the truck. "Get my shotgun", I thought. Too late, a buck ran out of the woods not thirty yards from us. Dan was clear to shoot once, missed; the deer was still running. Lord only knows why I had the presence of mind to whistle, but it worked. The buck stopped and looked back at the truck. Dan's second shot sent a slug into the buck's neck at 60 to 70 yards and it never got up.

Dan's comment, a shocked, "I'll be —? How did you do that? The thought came to me, "Luck, I guess" I answered.

Then and there, I thanked God again for the good fortune. Dan and I split the venison 50-50 from the "lucky" buck so both of our families enjoyed venison in 1984. Talk about two of the happiest buck hunters!

Been there and done that!

The Big One That Got Away

Once while deer hunting with a friend from Philadelphia, Mississippi just north of Meridian, Mississippi, I got a big chance to shoot a huge buck.

We heard a dog barking in the woods as we stood talking on a logging road. Greg said it sounded like the dog was on a deer trail and for us to spread out on the farm road for a crossing shot. I was

walking slowly and stopping to listen for a deer coming through the woods. I had walked about 50 to 60 yards when without warning a big deer jumped out of the thick brush along the side of the road 30 yards ahead of me. It bounded once in the middle of the logging road and then off into the hardwoods on the right. The deer caught me by surprise. The size of the huge deer with a huge rack shook me up for an instant, so my aim on the deer was slow and careful as I squeezed on the trigger.

My gun never fired and the deer got across the logging road and into the hardwoods before I had a killing shot. I never had an aim on his neck or lungs for a vital shot. It would have been possible to hit his hind quarter artery, I guess, if I had shot faster. But I didn't pull the trigger faster than normal. I guess I kept my composure. I didn't want to snap shoot and wound the deer and then lose him. I would have felt worse to wound and lose the deer than to have let it go for another hunt as I did. I'll have to live with that decision.

I hope that's not the only huge buck I get to shoot!! No venison for our family this season.

The Cautious 8 Point

Years ago I was one invited guest of a customer in Mississippi to hunt whitetail deer at their hunting lodge. We arranged to meet in town for a two day hunt. After loading my rifle and other gear into Steve's pick-up truck we were headed down dirt roads for an hour or so until we arrived at the lodge.

There were three of us customer deer hunters to be guided by Steve and Sherman. After getting introduced to the camp cook, Buddy, and unpacking our hunting gear we all were anxious to hunt the afternoon from the various deer stands we had to choose from. Steve and Sherman said they had been seeing bucks and does

coming into wheat and grass plots located near deer stands on the
south side of their property over the last two weeks or so. "That
sounds good enough to me", I commented. "Let me take any stand
over there." Last deer season I did not take a deer so my family was
anxious to have some fresh venison in our freezer. Getting a trophy
buck would even be better.

Sherman and Steve took the three of us guests to our deer
stands on four wheelers. We were to hunt until dark and they
would be back to pick us up. I liked my high, sturdy stand
overlooking a planted wheat field surrounded by thick woods. As
darkness neared the temperature seemed to drop like a rock and I
still had not seen the first deer. It was real quiet. A great time to be
in the woods, but I was praying for a buck to enter the field before
dark. That would be a case of beginners luck really. Seldom does it
happen where you deer hunt a new spot for two to three hours and
get a shot at a buck. So — I was wishful thinking.

Then, just before dark a deer without making a sound slipped
into the field to browse. Not seeing horns I raised my scoped 30-06
Remington Model 760 deer rifle to get a better look at the deer. No,
no horns on this one. Ten minutes later with the deer still in the
field I climbed down from the stand and waited for my taxi ride
back to camp. Then I heard a shot not far away. Hey, maybe one of
the other two guests was able to take a buck, I thought.

Back at camp I learned the other two guests were Larry and
Randy. Randy had a shot at a yearling spike buck right at dark and
had missed with his open sighted Winchester 30-30 from seventy-
five yards or so. Since we all had a morning, afternoon and a
morning still hunts from stands ahead of us, our hosts said we
could all get shots at bucks before our hunt ends in a couple of
days. I thought, "that kind of deer hunting would be unbelievable."

Buddy fixed us a very good meal that night. After some
storytelling and card playing we hit the sack with buck racks in
our dreams thanks to the buck tales told by hosts that evening.

We were all up before five a.m. since we all needed to be in our

various tree stands for watch well before first daylight. Steve suggested we each take our morning watch in new tree stand locations to help keep our spirits high. Wow, I liked the stand they chose for me. There was a great view of a soybean field from the back corner of the woods. The stand was solid, had a shooting rail to brace your rifle and a chair, too. We would be on stand watching for bucks only until lunch was delivered to us and then, it would be time to re-evaluate our afternoon hunting options.

It was a beautiful sunrise indeed. The temperature was about 20 degrees but going up to near 50 degrees later in the day. About 7:45 a.m. there was one shot fired nearby and I thought it had to be either Larry or Randy getting a shot. Was I envious? Yes, a little bit. When you hear one lone shot, it usually means the deer or buck in this case, was taken cleanly. Later I would hear the whole story.

Not one deer had as much as crossed my soybean field by the time Sherman brought my lunch. Sherman said that Larry had taken a nice six-point buck about 8:00. So I was right. Since I had not seen a deer we agreed to relocate me to a new deer stand for the afternoon watch.

This new stand was along a creek bank overlooking a rather small grass plot. Sherman said they have made ten stands like this after clearing and planting these feed plots for over eight years. "Just never know when a buck will show up to browse," said Sherman before leaving.

What a beautiful day to be in the woods. Sunny, warm, only a light breeze so now I only need a buck to show up to make the hunting seem complete. But as sunset was nearing my chances of taking a buck were lessening.

Then, I heard brush cracking as if a deer or two were running toward the field in front of me. The noise stopped for a minute or two, then more brush scraping sounds. Those woods must be really thick, I thought. The noisy movement went on and off until just before dark. Then two doe walked into the field, looked around and carefully began to browse.

To be sure the two deer were doe and one not being a spike buck, I put my rifle scope on each deer separately. About the time I whispered "No horns," another deer slipped onto the edge of the field. In the scope his long-tined rack was obvious. With my rifle resting on the deer stand rail I eased off the safety and aimed at the buck's vital shoulder area and fired. The buck leaped into the air and fell to the ground. I held for a second shot but the buck never moved and I thanked my Lord for the venison from another successful deer hunt.

A Deep South Deer Hunt

The 1985 deer hunting season saw me hunting two days of the muzzleloader season with Lane and his son Joe. It was rainy and cold those two days for the most part, but since we could shoot either sex deer, we wanted to hunt anyway despite the weather.

The first day was pretty tough hunting. That afternoon I had not seen a deer but Joe had turned down a shot at a doe with hopes to shoot a buck. Lane shot twice at a BIG buck but his caps would not fire his muzzleloader. The BIG buck walked away unharmed. The second morning Lane had a buck walk within 20 yards of him. Lane pulled the trigger of his percussion muzzleloader twice but the hammer each time never hit the cap. Again the deer walked off untouched. That second afternoon after returning for lunch at the truck with Joe and me, Lane showed us how his gun was not working right. He could not stop telling how nice a buck that he could have shot if it were not for his gun not firing. After lunch we figured out a way for him to shoot it. Then we all chose spots to sit on watch from 1:00 p.m. until dark. Lane was the first to leave on his four-wheeler. Joe and I were to follow and hunt the woods to the north of the clear cut.

A few minutes after Lane left we heard his muzzleloader go off. We wondered if it went off while carrying it on his four-wheeler and we were afraid he may have hurt himself. Joe and I ran down

the trail that Lane had taken. Then we stopped when we heard Lane coming back toward us on his four-wheeler.

Lane stopped his four-wheeler twenty feet away. Talk about broken up — he was crying and babbling. He threw his muzzleloader on the ground and said he was quitting. He had missed a spike buck not 15 yards away standing still in the open as it was eating on the side of the roadway. That does it!

In two days Lane had missed two big bucks and a spike horn. No venison for any of us — just sad memories! My wife will not like the bad news. No venison for us this year, Gale.

The Welcome Home Buck

In 1987 another promotion had us relocating from Meridian, Mississippi to a northern suburb of Philadelphia, Pennsylvania. The relocation brought us within five hours driving time of home. So after years, I was excited about being able to deer hunt familiar woods with old friends.

Two great things happened during my 1987 deer season. First, on the second day of the New York deer season I went to a spot in Fred Arliss' woods in Lock Pit, Clyde, New York that I had seen a month earlier during the duck season. I had found a buck scrape line along an access road to a huge alfalfa field. That day I had the urge to watch that scrape line from a vantage point at the end of the field.

I was sitting against a tree in the corner of the field about 4:00 p.m. when it started to drizzle rain. It was very windy and darkness was only 30 minutes away. Not a very good day for deer hunting because deer do not like windy days. It disrupts their hearing and sense of smell. Oh, well! Just do it!

A few minutes after I sat on watch I saw three or four deer running out of the woods and down the middle of the field toward the far end. Maybe ten minutes later, I guess, I could see one lone

deer come out of the woods straight across from me and begin crossing the field toward my end of the field. I wondered why it had not gone down toward the other end of the field like the other deer. I suppose it was looking for the other deer but did not know where they went and was coming my way to look for them. With the winds blowing it wasn't wasting time crossing the field. The deer was a long way off, but coming at me when it changed its angle. I saw something on its head sort of. I felt it had horns. So I sat up and steadied my Ithaca automatic shotgun against the other side of the tree and waited for the deer to cross into my waiting sights. Suddenly, the deer was there; I aimed at the front shoulder and fired, aimed and fired again. The buck jumped and jumped again into the woods this time. He's hit!

I was so excited I could not sit there very long. With my being able to rest the gun on the tree and have the deer walk into the sights, I felt confident in my shot placement. I should have stayed put for thirty minutes, but I could not because it was getting dark and raining. I did not want to lose this buck and I felt nervous about losing its blood trail. After only a few minutes I decided to trail the buck and hoped it was down for good.

I went to the approximate spot where the deer was when I shot to see if I could find a blood trail. I looked ahead in the trail's direction and there was my buck laying down. It was a big deer and was moving its head around. Then it saw me and bolted off. I took one shot straight away and I was out of slugs. Mistake! I was so excited I forgot to reload the two slugs I shot at the deer already. Off goes my wounded buck — —

I slowly reloaded and traipsed off after the buck but I could not find a blood trail to save my life. Getting darker and wetter by the minute, I was afraid I was going to lose my nice buck. Then, I heard a shot and then another nearby. I yelled, "I shot a buck. Did he run your way?" "Yes! He is over here," came back the answer.

Boy, I ran through brush to get there. I found one of our hunting crew standing near my deer. Dick said he missed his first

shot but the next one hit the deer in the back of the neck as it ran
by. It hit the ground and never moved. Dick saw the two holes in
the chest area that I put there and said, "It's your deer, Steve, I
just finished him off." Dick helped me field dress my buck, but I
had to drag it over 100 yards to the truck. It was a big heavy buck
and I really worked up a sweat.

I was so happy because I had not taken a buck in five seasons.
The deer had a small three-point rack but I don't care much about
eating deer racks anyway! I am always interested in venison first
and rack second. Thanks, Lord, for the venison!!

Beginner's Luck or The Big Buck That Did Not Get Away

The second great thing that happened during my 1987 deer
season happened up at Lake Nochimixon state game lands in
Pennsylvania. I was going to hunt the first Saturday of the
Pennsylvania season with Ed and Fred on the land where you
could take either a doe or a buck. Fred, a sales rep in our office who
had never been deer hunting, wanted to go along. I told Fred to get
his license during the week and I would pick him up at 5:30
Saturday morning. Friday night he called to say he had his license
and asked to borrow one of my shotguns and deer slugs.

Early the next morning I was up loading my hunting gear, our
guns and deer slugs in the car so I would not be late. At 5:00 a.m. I
picked up Ed and we were at Fred's home at 5:30 a.m. Fred was
excited because he was already waiting outside on the street for us
to arrive.

On the way to Nochimixon game lands Ed and I gave the
novice deer hunter in the back seat some tips on deer hunting and I
told Fred where to aim my double barrel Ithaca 12 gauge to stop a
deer with one deer slug. We left the car at 6:15 a.m. together and
went to the spot in the woods Ed knew of. There Ed left me and

took Fred to a spot nearby. At 10:00 a.m. Ed was to come by and get Fred and then come over to me and we'd call it a day.

There was alot of shooting near me that morning from 8 to 9:30 a.m. but I never even saw a deer. At 9:30 a.m. Ed came to get me and to help look for a doe he might have hit. After thirty minutes of looking, we decided he had missed it after all and it was time to find Fred. When we found Fred, it went like this:

"Fred, Fred, yah over here." As we got closer we asked if he saw anything. Fred says, "Yah, I got one!" Did he get one! Ed and I could see the big horns up off the ground from a distance of over 50 yards through the grass. Fred dropped the buck with one 12 gauge slug into the deer's front shoulder near the neck. Right where we told him to aim.

Wow, what a nice buck with a perfect eight-point symmetrical rack. Talk about a pretty rack. We were all thrilled about Fred's buck. Ed and I did most of the field dressing of the buck. Fred and I dragged the deer out to my car where Fred returned my gun and my extra slugs that were appreciated but no longer needed. We took pictures of the deer and Fred with my camera before leaving for home with the deer in my trunk.

We went by Nochimixon Sporting Goods. Walt took pictures of Fred and his buck and measured its horns for Boone and Crocket points. It had a 20 inch spread and scored 145 points.

Beginner's luck? Certainly was — it happens in deer hunting! Want to see the pictures?

With Steve's big game hunting knife in hand, he is about to show his "beginner's luck," Fred Florian, how to cape his trophy 8-point whitetail deer for mounting. If that is not bad enough, Steve later drove him and the cape to the very best taxidermist in our area so the mounting would be done right.

Hey, does this look like <u>one very happy</u> whitetail deer hunter to you? In his first deer hunt Fred is overjoyed at taking his 8-point trophy buck and looking forward to sharing its nutritiously delicious venison with his family, too. We all enjoyed the venison filet mignon and some tenderloin grilled to perfection in a celebration meal that night. What a memory…

Index

D

E

F

G

H

T

V

VENISON HOW-TO-GUIDE:

VENISON ITALIAN STYLE:

Quality Venison II

All New Recipes And Deer Tales Too...

Quality Venison II contains 150 new user-friendly, "cook's-style" recipes plus two new recipe sections - Cooking Venison Southern Style and Preparing Venison Marinades and Sauces. Put together with the same care and attention to detail as our first book, this title will expand your collection of mouth-watering venison dishes. To start, you'll want to try: "Easy Deer Camp Venison Roast," "Appalachian Mountain Sauce," "Rebel Yell Hot Barbecue Sauce" and "Chunky Venison Pasta Bake." There are so many great tastes here, you'll be in the kitchen for days, and your family and friends will applaud the results.

It was published in 1999, 192 pages, 6x9, comb bound with a lay-flat hard cover.

Quality Venison III

All New Wild Game Recipes And Hunting Tales Too...

Over 100 new taste-tested and user friendly recipes for venison and other wild game, including appetizers and side dishes to complement the wild game dishes you prepare! Also, for your reading pleasure when you are not cooking our deliciously nutritious wild game meals for your family and friends, we have created an extended Hunting Tales section of two dozen tales written by Steve and several other featured hunters and outdoor writers. Based on our book sales success of *Quality Venison* and *Quality Venison II* we can guarantee you will like the way we have painstakingly written *Quality Venison III*.

It was published in 2002, 224 pages, 6x9, comb bound with a lay-flat hard cover.

Order your copies today by using the handy order form on the facing page, or simply send $16.95 plus $3.50 postage and handling per copy (Pennsylvania residents add $1.23 sales tax) to:

Loders' Game Publications

P.O. Box 1615 • Cranberry Township, PA 16066

Loders' Game Publications, Inc.

P.O. Box 1615, Cranberry Township, Pennsylvania 16066
Phone: (724) 779-8320

Please send _____ copies of *Quality Venison*   @ $16.95 each _____

Please send _____ copies of *Quality Venison II*   @ $16.95 each _____

Please send _____ copies of *Quality Venison III*   @ $16.95 each _____

         Postage and handling   @ $ 3.50 each _____

         Pennsylvania residents, add sales tax   @ $ 1.23 each _____

         Total _____

Make checks payable to: **Loders' Game Publications, Inc.**

Name _____

Address _____

City _____ State _____ Zip _____

Phone (day) _____ (night) _____

❏   Please keep me informed of future wild game publications

Loders' Game Publications, Inc.

P.O. Box 1615, Cranberry Township, Pennsylvania 16066
Phone: (724) 779-8320

Please send _____ copies of *Quality Venison*   @ $16.95 each _____

Please send _____ copies of *Quality Venison II*   @ $16.95 each _____

Please send _____ copies of *Quality Venison III*   @ $16.95 each _____

         Postage and handling   @ $ 3.50 each _____

         Pennsylvania residents, add sales tax   @ $ 1.23 each _____

         Total _____

Make checks payable to: **Loders' Game Publications, Inc.**

Name _____

Address _____

City _____ State _____ Zip _____

Phone (day) _____ (night) _____

❏   Please keep me informed of future wild game publications

Here's What People Are Saying About
QUALITY VENISON

"When I ordered your first book I enclosed a note indicating that all I needed now was a deer (which I had not harvested for a couple of years.) You responded (I don't remember the exact words) that I should have patience and persevere. Well the red gods smiled on me and I harvested a fine (10-point) buck next season (my personal all time best.) I had an opportunity to try some of your recipes and I liked them all. I especially enjoy your hunting stories. It is refreshing to read that I am not the only one to hunt all day (or all season) and not get a shot. I too have experienced misses, adverse weather, and yes, I too have experienced the heart break of failure to recover a wounded animal (only once.) And finally, yes, I am a "meat hunter" and proud of it. Good luck to you in the upcoming season(s)."

Fellow deer hunter and customer, Reading, PA

"Enclosed is a money order for a copy of *Quality Venison III*. I love your books so much I have bought a second copy of each as gifts for a friend. I think *Quality Venison III* is your best yet! I enjoy your writings as much as I do your great recipes. Can't wait for *Quality Venison IV*."

Ron Carlisle, Pittsburgh, PA

"Please send Book I and Book II to the address above. I was going to purchase these books for my son, but after speaking to you, I think I'll use them for now, and leave them to him in my will!!!" When giving us permission to use her testimonial, Susan remarked, "I love the books."

Susan E. Hilliard, Butler, PA

"Earl and I have tried several of your recipes and every one has been delicious! This morning we cooked a small buffalo roast using 'Dad's Onion Roasted Venison,'" (Book I, page 112.) "It just came out of the oven. Yum! don't really want to share it but we already told the "kids" we'd bring it out for a football eat-in. We just wanted you all (yaw'l) to know we've enjoyed your first two cookbooks and waiting for the third."

Earl and Margaret Coppage, Lynchburg, VA

When ordering one each of our first two *Quality Venison* cookbooks, Mrs. Schlosser commented, "Book II is a gift to our son and his wife. They talked about ordering this book. Hopefully my order will arrive before they decide to order! We use Book I and haven't found a recipe yet that we didn't like!" When Mrs. Schlosser mailed us her permission to use her testimonial she was kind enough to comment that their favorite recipe in Book I is "Crock Pot Venison Burgundy" found on page 91.

Mary Ann Schlosser, Rib Lake, WI

"We loved our copy so much we want to order some for friends. They make great gifts! I knew from the minute I saw the cover that this was a book my husband would love. He loved it so much I ordered several more copies to give to friends as gifts. Your book should be on every hunter's shelf."

Mary Mauk, Summerville, PA

"Please send two more copies of the *Quality Venison* cookbook. I have ordered one for myself and I have enjoyed it so much that I would like to give these two as Christmas gifts. Thank you."

David Jost, Borger, TX

"Enclosed is a check for three Loder's cookbooks. I gave my husband one for Christmas and he enjoys it so much he wants to give one to his three hunting buddies. Thank you."

Dorothy and Mike Comerford, Seneca Falls, NY

"Thank you for taking the time to put together a wonderful venison cookbook. I bought it for my youngest son who is a father and loves to hunt and fish like his father did. The stories were great and reminded me of my husband who loved to hunt and fish in Pennsylvania, Maryland, West Virginia and Virginia. I'm ordering more books for family members. What great gifts. God bless."

Frances Augustine, Alexandria, VA

"I am sending this outstanding cookbook to my father who taught me the love for the outdoors. My wife has been very impressed with how tasty 'my cooking' has been. Thanks for the recipes, which allow me to enjoy my hunting experiences year round. My employees at work love when I cook crockpot recipes at the shop. My mother is going to purchase a couple cookbooks, too. She loves venison."

Gerry Smerka, Jr., Hamden, CT

"I'm writing you to compliment you on your venison cookbook, *Quality Venison*. My wife bought it for me for Christmas and we have used several recipes and marked all the ones we used with **very good**. As a matter of fact, I'm going to use Pittsburgh Venison Loin for the main meal at my game dinner. It's simple, it's quick and it's delicious."

Graham Hoffman, Canandaigua, NY

"You have a great book! I left my first book from you in our Southern home and I need one for Pennsylvania! Have cooked many of your recipes. I love Deer now! Please send extra order forms for our friends in the NRA. I told them the book would be a great prize for their yearly banquets."

Darla J. Clark, Belle Vernon, PA

"Do you remember my rather anxious call when my husband, Rege, and I were attempting to butcher our first deer? We didn't get very far because the carcass cavity had a suspiciously spoiled odor about it. You suggested we allowed it to hang too long and gave us some invaluable advice. (We decided to discard that one, much to our chagrin). Several weeks later Rege, his dad, and his brother shot (3) doe at camp in the Cook Forest, PA area. With your book and advice we butchered all (3) deer and were quite pleased with the results. And all of it is delicious! Deboned, de-fatted and double wrapped! Thank you for your personal advice and your book. We couldn't have done it without you! And your recipes, specifically for venison, are a rare find."

Connie Gmuer, Rock Cave, WV

"Recently I purchased your cookbook, *Quality Venison*. I was delighted to have found it—will make a terrific Christmas gift for our daughter's boyfriend, who is quite a hunter. Michael really likes to cook, and your book is not only full of mouthwatering recipes, but wonderful tips and stories as well—know he will enjoy it. Once again, thank you for your wonderful cookbook—it is 'very' well done. One can see that you put much effort and thought into it."

Judy Walters, Sayre, PA

"Last Christmas my mom bought your cookbook for me. I just wanted to pass along how much I have appreciated it. It is a fun book with valuable information. Your tips on processing have been taken into practice. Although the information is great the greatest blessing in the book is your love for Jesus Christ. Thank you for your encouragement."

Bill Daugherty, Renfrew, PA

"My wife and I have used your first book since December of 1998. We find the recipes great. This year was the first year I harvested two deer, and we followed your book in processing our second deer and did everything ourselves. What a feeling of accomplishment. Thanks."

Roger J. Weber, Lehighton, PA

"Just got *Quality Venison I* and need to tell you that we really enjoy your collection of recipes. Please send my *Quality Venison II* as soon as you can so that I may try others. Don't want to miss out on anything. Thank you."

Louise J. Burke, Smock, PA

"My name is Scott Miller from Des Moines, IA. We spoke briefly on the phone today in regards to ordering your book, *Quality Venison, Homemade Recipes & Homespun Deer Tales*. It is a book I believe every deer hunter should not be without. I admire your respect for the whitetail, God bless you and your family."

Scott Miller, Des Moines, IA

"My daughter is always borrowing my venison cookbook (*Quality Venison*), so I figure I may as well buy her one. I can't tell you how much we enjoy our venison since I bought *Quality Venison*. Thank you for a wonderful book."

R. Evelyn Krueger, Danville, PA

"I 'lost' my first copy to my brother. We think it's great! Thank you."

Michaelene Geiser, Binghamton, NY

(Michaelene bought two more copies of *Quality Venison*)

"I tried one of your venison steak recipes that was in the Beaver newspaper. *Outstanding*. My seven year old daughter, who was rapidly becoming an anti-hunter, took one bite and said, 'Dad, go shoot another deer!' Please send me a copy of your venison cookbook to the above address. Enclosed is a check. Thanks much."

Bryan Bly, Beaver Falls, PA

"We talked on the phone last month. I had seen your cookbook ad in a hunting magazine. I ordered two of your cookbooks for family members. THEY EXCEEDED MY EXPECTATIONS. NICE WORK. Attached is an order and check for 2 more cookbooks. Please send them as quickly as you can as I need them for Christmas gifts. And let me know about future opportunities."

Gerald Schoonover, Middleburg, FL

"I received your book as a gift and, after skimming through it last night for an hour or two, I decided I just had to order it for my dad for his up-coming birthday. Your book is excellent from the cover right on through. You had me cooking up some venison loin steaks at 1:30 in the morning last night."

H. Eric Van Leer, Skaneateles, NY

"We received your cookbook for *Quality Venison* and are delighted. Such a nice hard covered cookbook for the price. We would like to order two more for gifts to our venison lovers. Also, we thank you for prompt shipping, no waiting 6-8 weeks for delivery is great."

Kenneth and Dorothy Jones, Canandaigua, NY

"I love the recipe book. I haven't had a chance to try a lot of the recipes but have made the 'Winter Venison Soup' on several occasions, usually sharing it with friends. Many have asked for the recipe. Reading the book has been a joy. I also gave a book as a special gift to a friend and felt I was giving a very useful and thoughtful gift. You have developed a treasure in this recipe book. Thank you."

Judy Brehm, Springwater, NY